Who Should Read This Book?

We've all heard the scenario: the family on vacation stops at a road-side "dig your own" gem mine. Junior finds a sapphire the size of a peach and ends up on national television telling the world how he will spend his fortune.

T This book is for those who have read these stories and want their chance to find their own fortune. It is also a book for those who would enjoy the adventure of finding a few gems, getting them cut or polished, and making their own jewelry. It is a book for those people who want to plan a gem hunting vacation with their family. It is a book for those who study the metaphysical properties of gems and minerals and would like to add to their personal collections.

T This book is for those who would like to keep the art of rock-hounding alive and pass it on to their children. It is a book on where to find your own gems and minerals and on how to begin what for many is a lifelong hobby.

T This is a book for those who aren't interested in the "hidden treasure map through mosquito-infested no-man's-land" approach to treasure hunting but do want to find gems and minerals. It is for those who want to get out the pick and shov-el and get a little dirty. (Although at some mines they bring the buckets of pre-dug dirt to you at an environmentally temper-ature controlled sluicing area.)

Many an unsuspecting tourist has stopped at a mine to try his or her luck and become a rockhound for life. Watch out! Your collection may end up taking the place of your car in your garage.

Good hunting!

This volume is one in a four-volume series.

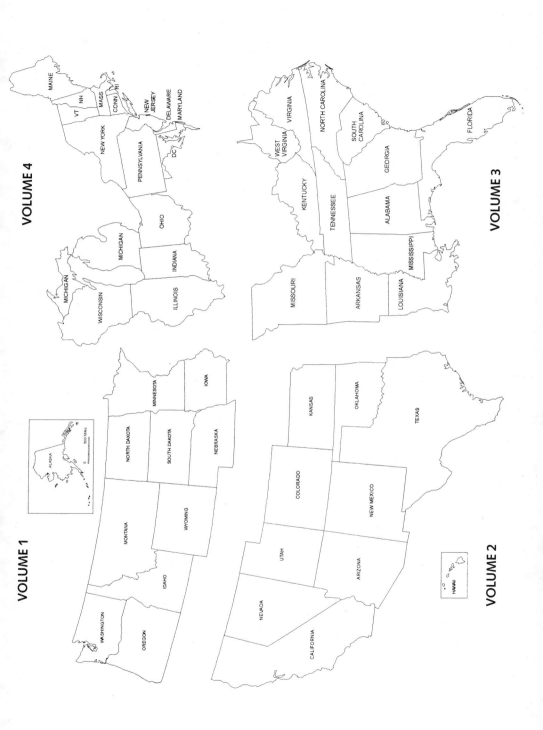

VOLUME 1

VOLUME 2

VOLUME 3

VOLUME 4

ALASKA

500 Miles

WASHINGTON
OREGON
IDAHO
MONTANA
WYOMING
NORTH DAKOTA
SOUTH DAKOTA
MINNESOTA
NEBRASKA
IOWA
KANSAS
OKLAHOMA
TEXAS
NEVADA
CALIFORNIA
UTAH
ARIZONA
COLORADO
NEW MEXICO

HAWAII

MISSOURI
ARKANSAS
LOUISIANA
MISSISSIPPI
ALABAMA
GEORGIA
FLORIDA
TENNESSEE
KENTUCKY
WEST VIRGINIA
VIRGINIA
NORTH CAROLINA
SOUTH CAROLINA

MICHIGAN
WISCONSIN
MICHIGAN
ILLINOIS
INDIANA
OHIO
PENNSYLVANIA
NEW YORK
MAINE
VT
NH
MASS
CONN RI
NEW JERSEY
DELAWARE
MARYLAND
DC

The Treasure Hunter's

GEM & MINERAL
GUIDES TO THE U.S.A.

3RD EDITION

Where & How to Dig, Pan, and Mine
Your Own Gems & Minerals

VOLUME 2: SOUTHWEST STATES

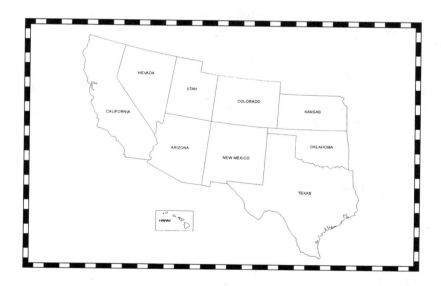

by KATHY J. RYGLE AND STEPHEN F. PEDERSEN
Preface by Antoinette Matlins, P.G.,
author of *Gem Identification Made Easy*

GEMSTONE PRESS
Woodstock, Vermont

The Treasure Hunter's Gem & Mineral Guides to the U.S.A.: 3rd Edition
Where & How to Dig, Pan and Mine Your Own Gems & Minerals
Volume 2: Southwest States

2006 Third Edition
© 2006 by Kathy J. Rygle and Stephen F. Pedersen

2003 Second Edition
1999 First Edition

Preface © 2006 by Antoinette Matlins

For information regarding permission to reprint material from this book, please mail or fax your request in writing to GemStone Press, Permissions Department, at the address / fax number listed below, or e-mail your request to permissions@gemstonepress.com.

The Library of Congress has cataloged the second edition as follows:

Rygle, Kathy J., 1955–
Southwest treasure hunter's gem & mineral guide : where & how to dig, pan, and mine your own gems & minerals / Kathy J. Rygle and Stephen F. Pedersen—2nd ed.
p.   cm.
Rev. ed. of: The treasure hunter's gem & mineral guides to the U.S.A. c1999.
Includes index.
ISBN 0-943763-37-1 (NW)—ISBN 0-943763-40-1 (SE)—
ISBN 0-943763-38-X (SW)—ISBN 0-943763-39-8 (NE)
1.   Minerals—Collection   and   preservation—United   States—Guidebooks.
2.   Precious   stones—Collection   and   preservation—United   States—Guidebooks.
3. United States—Guidebooks. I. Pedersen, Stephen F., 1948– II. Rygle, Kathy J., 1955– Treasure hunter's gem & mineral guides to the U.S.A. III. Title.
QE375.R92 2003
549.973—dc21

2003040801

ISBNs for third edition:
ISBN-13: 978-0-943763-48-4(NW)   ISBN-13: 978-0-943763-50-7(SW)
ISBN-10: 0-943763-48-7(NW)   ISBN-10: 0-943763-50-9(SW)
ISBN-13: 978-0-943763-49-1(NE)   ISBN-13: 978-0-943763-51-4(SE)
ISBN-10: 0-943763-49-5(NE)   ISBN-10: 0-943763-51-7(SE)

Cover design by Bronwen Battaglia
Text design by Chelsea Dippel

10   9   8   7   6   5   4   3   2   1

Manufactured in the United States of America

Published by GemStone Press
A Division of LongHill Partners, Inc.
Sunset Farm Offices, Route 4, P.O. Box 237
Woodstock, VT 05091
Tel: (802) 457-4000   Fax: (802) 457-4004
www.gemstonepress.com

Dedications, with love, to our parents and children:

To my parents, Joe and Helen Rygle, who taught me the love of nature; my earliest remembrances of "rockhounding" are hikes with my dad in the fields, forests, and streams near our home. I also remember weekend trips with my mother to a shop that sold specimens of minerals from around the world. To my daughter, Annie Rygle, who shares with me and continues to show me the wonders of nature. Also, thanks to Annie for helping me sort the information for the updates.   —K. J. R.

To my parents, Cliff and Leone Pedersen, who taught me to value nature and to not quit. To my daughters Kristi and Debbie, who challenge me to keep growing.   —S. F. P.

To our combined families, including Georgia Pedersen, and to family no longer with us.

With special thanks:

To all the owners of fee dig mines and guide services, curators and staff of public and private museums, mine owners, and miners. Our thanks to all those individuals both past and present who share the wonders of the earth with us.

To our agent, Barb Doyen, and her childhood rock collection.

To our publisher, Stuart M. Matlins, editor Emily Wichland, and all the staff at GemStone Press for their guidance, assistance, and patience.

To Mrs. Betty Jackson for, in her own way, telling Kathy to write the book.

To God and the wonders He has given us.

And finally, to each other, with love and the perseverance to keep on trying.

Volume 2—Southwest States

CONTENTS

All-American Gems

by Antoinette Matlins, P.G.

When Americans think of costly and fabled gems, they associate them with exotic origins—Asia, South Africa or Brazil. They envision violent jungle quests or secret cellars of a sultanate, perhaps scenes from a Jorge Amado novel or from *A Thousand and One Nights*, a voluptuous Indian princess whose sari is adorned with the plentiful rubies and sapphires of her land, or a Chinese emperor sitting atop a throne flanked by dragons carved from exquisitely polished jade.

Asked what gems are mined in the United States, most Americans would probably draw a blank. We know our country is paved with one of the finest highway systems in the world, but we don't know that just below the surface, and sometimes on top of it, is a glittering pavement of gemstones that would color Old Glory. The red rubies of North Carolina, the white diamonds of Arkansas, the blue sapphires of Montana—America teems with treasures that its citizens imagine come from foreign lands. These include turquoise, tourmaline, amethyst, pearls, opals, jade, sapphires, emeralds, rubies, and even gem-quality diamonds.

Not only does America have quantity, it has quality. American gems compare very favorably with gems from other countries. In fact, fine gemstones found in the U.S. can rival specimens from anywhere else in the world. Some gems, like the luxurious emerald-green hiddenite and steely blue benitoite, are found only in America. Others, like the tourmalines of Maine and California, rival specimens found in better-known locations such as Brazil and Zambia.

The discovery of gemstones in U.S. terrain has been called a lost chapter in American history. It continues to be a saga of fashion and fable that, like the stones themselves, are a deep part of our national heritage. Appreciation of our land's generous yield of sparkling colored stones reached a zenith at the end of the nineteenth century with the art nouveau movement and its utilization of them. When the Boer Wars ended, South Africa's diamonds and platinum eclipsed many of our own then so-called semiprecious stones. Not until the 1930s, and again starting with the 1960s, did economics and the yen for color make gems more desirable again.

In the late 1800s, the nation sought out and cherished anything that was unique to the land. The search for gemstones in America coincided with the exploration of the West, and nineteenth-century mineralogists, some bonafide and others self-proclaimed, fulfilled that first call for "Made in America." Their discoveries created sensations not only throughout America but in the capitals of Europe and as far away as China. The Europeans, in fact, caught on before the Americans, exhibiting some of America's finest specimens in many of Europe's great halls.

But the search for gemstones in this country goes back even further than the nineteenth century. In 1541, the Spanish explorer Francisco Coronado trekked north from Mexico in the footsteps of Cortés and Pizarro, searching not only for gold but also for turquoise, amethyst and emeralds. In the early 1600s, when English settlers reached Virginia, they had been instructed "to searche for gold and such jewels as ye may find."

But what eluded the Spanish explorers and early settlers was unearthed by their descendants. Benitoite, which may be our nation's most uniquely attractive gem, was discovered in 1907 in California's San Benito River headwaters. A beautiful, rare gem with the color of fine sapphire and the fire of a diamond, benitoite is currently found in gem quality only in San Benito, California.

Like many of America's finest stones discovered during the "Gem Rush" of the nineteenth century, benitoite was held in higher regard throughout the rest of the world than it was on its native U.S. soil.

The gem occurs most commonly in various shades of blue. A fine-quality blue benitoite can resemble fine blue sapphire, but it is even more brilliant. It has one weakness, however: in comparison to sapphire, it is relatively soft. It is therefore best used in pendants, brooches and earrings, or in rings with a protective setting.

While benitoite is among the rarest of our gems, our riches hardly stop there. America is the source of other unusual gems, including three even more uniquely American stones, each named after an American: kunzite, hiddenite and morganite.

The story of all-American kunzite is inseparable from the achievements of two men: Charles Lewis Tiffany, founder of Tiffany & Co., and Dr. George Frederick Kunz, world-renowned gemologist. By seeking, collecting and promoting gems found in America, these two did more for the development of native stones than anyone else during, or since, their time.

While working for Tiffany in the late 1800s, Dr. Kunz received a package in the mail containing a stone that the sender believed to be an unusual tourmaline. The stone came from an abandoned mine at Pala Mountain, California, where collectors had found traces of spodumene—a gemstone prized by the ancients but which no one had been able to find for many years. Dr. Kunz was ecstatic to find before him a specimen of "extinct spodumene of a gloriously lilac color." A fellow gemologist, Dr. Charles Baskerville, named the find "kunzite" in his honor.

Kunzite has become a favorite of such designers as Paloma Picasso, not only because of its distinctive shades—lilac, pink, and yellow-green orchid—but because it is one of a diminishing number of gems available in very large sizes at affordable prices. It is a perfect choice for the centerpiece around which to create a very bold, dramatic piece of jewelry. Designer Picasso's creations include a magnificent necklace using a 400-carat kunzite. Although it is a moderately hard stone, kunzite is easily fractured, and care must be taken to avoid any sharp blows.

Kunzite's sister gem, hiddenite, is also a truly "all-American" stone. In 1879, William Earl Hidden, an engraver and mineralogist, was sent to North Carolina on behalf of the great American inventor and prospector Thomas Alva Edison to search for platinum. Hidden found none of the precious white metal but in his pursuit unearthed a new green gemstone, which was named "hiddenite" in his honor.

Less well known than kunzite, hiddenite is an exquisite, brilliant emerald-green variety of spodumene not found anyplace else in the world. While light green and yellow-green shades have been called hiddenite, the Gemological Institute of America—this country's leading authority on gemstones—considers only the emerald-green shade of spodumene, found exclusively in the Blue Ridge Mountains of Mitchell County, North Carolina, to be true hiddenite.

The foothills of the Blue Ridge Mountains also possess America's most significant emerald deposits. While output is minimal compared to Colombia, Zambia or Pakistan, the Rist Mine in Hiddenite, North Carolina, has produced some very fine emeralds, comparable to Colombian stones. The discovery was first made by a farmer plowing his field who found them lying loose on the soil. The country folk, not knowing what they had come across, called the stones "green bolts."

In August 1970, a 26-year-old "rock hound" named Wayne Anthony found a glowing 59-carat "green bolt" at the Rist Mine only two feet from the surface. It was cut into a 13.14-carat emerald of very fine color. Tiffany & Co. later purchased the stone and called it the Carolina Emerald. "The gem is superb," said Paul E. Desautels, then the curator of mineralogy at the Smithsonian Institution. "It can stand on its own merits as a fine and lovely gem of emerald from anywhere, including Colombia." In 1973, the emerald became the official state stone of North Carolina.

A California prize, the warm peach- or pink-shaded morganite, was named by Dr. Kunz for financier John Pierpont Morgan, who purchased the Bement gem collection for donation to the American Museum of Natural History in New York, where it can be viewed today. Morganite is a member of the beryl family, which gives us aquamarine (the clear blue variety of beryl) and emerald (the deep green variety of beryl). However, morganite is available in much larger sizes than its mineralogical cousins and is much more affordable.

Many consider the core of our national treasure chest to be gems like the tourmalines of Maine and California and the sapphires of Montana, gems that are mined in commercial quantities and have earned worldwide reputations. One day in the fall of 1820, two young boys, Ezekiel Holmes and Elijah Hamlin, were rock hunting on Mount Mica in Oxford County, Maine. On the way home, one of the boys saw a flash of green light coming from underneath an uprooted tree. The find was later identified as tourmaline, and Mount Mica became the site of the first commercial gem mine in the United States. The mine was initially worked by Elijah Hamlin and his brother Hannibal, who later became Abraham Lincoln's vice president.

The colors of the rainbow meld delicately in the tourmalines of Maine, producing some of the finest specimens in the world, rivaling in quality even those from Brazil. A 150-mile strip in central Maine provides shades of apple green, burgundy red and salmon pink, to mention just a few. Some stones are bi-colored.

Miners are kept busy in the Pala district of San Diego County, California, as well. California, in fact, is North America's largest producer of gem-quality tourmaline.

The hot-pink tourmalines, for which California is famous, began to come into greater demand in 1985, as pastel-colored stones became more and more coveted by chic women around the globe. Curiously enough, over one hundred years ago the Chinese rejoiced in the fabulous colors of this fashionable stone. The Empress Dowager of the Last Chinese Imperial Dynasty sent emissaries to California in search of pink tourmalines. She garnished her robes with carved tourmaline buttons and toggles, and started a fad which overtook China. Much of the empress's collection of fine carvings was lost or stolen when the dynasty fell around 1912, but artifacts made from California's pink tourmaline can be seen today in a Beijing museum. China's fascination with pink tourmalines lasted long after the empress. In 1985, a contingent of the Chinese Geological Survey came to California with two requests: to see Disneyland and the Himalaya Mine, original site of California pink tourmaline.

While the Chinese are mesmerized by our tourmalines, Americans have always been attracted to China's jade. But perhaps we ought to take stock of our own. Wyoming, in fact, is the most important producer of the stone in the Western Hemisphere. The state produces large quantities of good-quality green nephrite jade—the type most commonly used in jewelry and carvings. California also boasts some jade, as does Alaska. Chinese immigrants panning for gold in California in the late 1800s found large boulders of nephrite and sent them back to China, where the jade was carved and sold within China and around the world.

The U.S. is also one of the largest producers of turquoise. Americans mostly associate this stone with American Indian jewelry, but its use by mainstream designers has regularly come in and out of fashion.

Some of the most prized gems of America are the stunning sapphires from Yogo Gulch, Montana. These sapphires emit a particularly pleasing shade of pale blue, and are known for their clarity and brilliance.

The Montana mine was originally owned by a gold-mining partnership. In 1895, an entire summer's work netted a total of only $700 in gold plus a cigar box full of heavy blue stones. The stones were sent to Tiffany & Co. to be identified. Tiffany then sent back a check for $3,750 for the entire box of obviously valuable stones.

Once one can conceive of gem-quality sapphires in America, it takes only a small stretch of the mind to picture the wonderful diamonds found here. A 40.23-carat white gem found in Murfreesboro, Arkansas, was cut into a 14.42-carat emerald-cut diamond named Uncle Sam. Other large diamonds include a 23.75-carat diamond found in the mid-nineteenth century in Manchester, Virginia, and a greenish 34.46-carat diamond named the Punch Jones, which was claimed to have been found in Peterstown, West Virginia.

Each year, thousands of people visit Crater of Diamonds State Park in Arkansas, where, for a fee, they can mine America's only proven location of gem-quality diamonds. Among them is a group known as "regulars" who visit the park looking for their "retirement stone."

In 1983, one of the regulars, 82-year-old Raymond Shaw, came across a 6.7-carat rough diamond. He sold it for $15,000 uncut. According to Mark Myers, assistant superintendent of the state park, the stone was cut into an exceptionally fine, 2.88-carat gem (graded E/Flawless by the Gemological Institute of America). Myers says the cut stone, later called the Shaw Diamond, was offered for sale for $58,000.

Diamonds have also been found along the shores of the Great Lakes, in many localities in California, in the Appalachian Mountains, in Illinois, Indiana, Ohio, Kentucky, New York, Idaho and Texas. Exploration for diamonds continues in Michigan, Wisconsin, Colorado and Wyoming, according to the U.S. Bureau of Mines. The discovery of gem-quality diamonds in Alaska in 1986 initiated a comprehensive search there for man's most valued gem.

Many questions concerning this country's store of gems remain unanswered. "Numerous domestic deposits of semiprecious gem stones are known and have been mined for many years," wrote the Bureau of Mines in a 1985 report. "However, no systematic evaluations of the magnitude of these deposits have been made and no positive statements can be made about them." Even as the United States continues to offer up its kaleidoscopic range of gems, our American soil may hold a still greater variety and quantity of gems yet to be unearthed.

And here, with the help of these down-to-earth (in the best possible way!)

guides, you can experience America's gem and mineral riches for yourself. In these pages rockhounds, gemologists, vacationers, and families alike will find a hands-on introduction to the fascinating world of gems and minerals . . . and a treasure map to a sparkling side of America. Happy digging!

T

Antoinette Matlins, P.G. is the most widely read author in the world on the subject of jewelry and gems (*Jewelry & Gems: The Buying Guide* alone has almost 400,000 copies in print). Her books are published in six languages and are widely used throughout the world by consumers and professionals in the gem and jewelry fields. An internationally respected gem and jewelry expert and a popular media guest, she is frequently quoted as an expert source in print media and is seen on ABC, CBS, NBC and CNN, educating the public about gems and jewelry and exposing fraud. In addition, Matlins is active in the gem trade. Her books include *Jewelry & Gems: The Buying Guide; Jewelry & Gems at Auction: The Definitive Guide to Buying & Selling at the Auction House & on Internet Auction Sites; Colored Gemstones: The Antoinette Matlins Buying Guide—How to Select, Buy, Care for & Enjoy Sapphires, Emeralds, Rubies and Other Colored Gems with Confidence and Knowledge; Diamonds: The Antoinette Matlins Buying Guide—How to Select, Buy, Care for & Enjoy Diamonds with Confidence and Knowledge; Engagement & Wedding Rings: The Definitive Buying Guide for People in Love; The Pearl Book: The Definitive Buying Guide;* and *Gem Identification Made Easy: A Hands-On Guide to More Confident Buying & Selling* (all GemStone Press).

Introduction

This is a guide to commercially operated gem and mineral mines (fee dig mines) within the United States that offer would-be treasure hunters the chance to "dig their own," from diamonds to thundereggs.

For simplicity, the term *fee dig site* is used to represent all types of fee-based mines or collection sites. However, for liability reasons, many mines no longer let collectors dig their own dirt, but rather dig it for them and provide it in buckets or bags. Some fee-based sites involve surface collection.

This book got its start when the authors, both environmental scientists, decided to make their own wedding rings. Having heard stories about digging your own gems, they decided to dig their own stones for their rings. So off to Idaho and Montana they went, taking their three children, ages 8, 13, and 15 at the time, in search of opals and garnets, their birthstones. They got a little vague information before and during the trip on where to find gem mines and in the process got lost in some of those "mosquito-infested lands." But when they did find actual "dig your own" mines (the kind outlined in this book), they found opals, garnets, and even sapphires. They have since made other trips to fee dig mines and each time have come home with treasures and some incredible memories.

The authors are also now the proud owners of a set of lapidary equipment, i.e., rock saw and rock polisher. They first used them to cut thundereggs collected from a mine in Oregon. The next project was to trim the many pounds of fossil fish rocks they acquired at a fee dig fossil site. The sequel to this guide series will cover authorized fossil collecting sites as well as museums on fossils and dinosaurs. It will include such topics as where to view and even make plaster casts of actual dinosaur tracks. There are even museums where kids of all ages can dig up a full-sized model of a dinosaur!

Types of Sites

The purpose of this book is principally to guide the reader to fee dig mine sites. These are gem or mineral mines where you hunt for the gem or mineral in ore at or from the mine. At fee dig sites where you are actually permitted to go into the field and dig for yourself, you will normally be shown what the gem or mineral you are seeking looks like in its natural state (much different from the polished or cut stone). Often someone is available to go out in the field with you and show you where to dig. At sites where you purchase gem- or mineral-bearing ore (either native or enriched) for washing in a flume, the process is the same: there will usually be examples of rough stones for comparison, and help in identifying your finds.

Also included are a few areas that are not fee dig sites but that are well-defined collecting sites, usually parks or beaches.

Guided field trips are a little different. Here the guide may or may not have examples of what you are looking for, but he or she will be with you in the field to help in identifying finds.

For the more experienced collector, there are field collecting areas where you are on your own in identifying what you have found. Several fee areas and guided field trips appropriate for the experienced collector are available. Check out the listings for Ruggles Mine (Grafton, NH); Harding Mine (Dixon, NM); Poland Mining Camps (Poland, ME); Perhams (West Paris, ME); and Gem Mountain Quarry Trips (Spruce Pine, NC).

Knowing What You're Looking For

Before you go out into the field, it is a good idea to know what you are looking for. Most of the fee dig mines listed in this guide will show you specimens before you set out to find your own. If you are using a guide service, you have the added bonus of having a knowledgeable person with you while you search to help you find the best place to look and help you identify your finds.

Included here is a listing of museums that contain rock and gem exhibits. A visit to these museums will help prepare you for your search. You may find examples of gems in the rough and examples of mineral specimens similar to the ones you will be looking for. Museums will most likely have displays of gems or minerals native to the local area. Some of the gems and minerals listed in this guide are of significant interest, and specimens of them can be found in museums around the country. Displays accompanying the exhibits might tell you how the gems and minerals were found, and their place in our nation's history. Many museums also hold collecting field trips or geology programs, or may be able to put you in touch with local rock and lapidary clubs.

For more information on learning how to identify your finds yourself—and even how to put together a basic portable "lab" to use at the sites—the book *Gem Identification Made Easy* by Antoinette Matlins and A. C. Bonanno (GemStone Press) is a good resource.

Rock shops are another excellent place to view gem and mineral specimens before going out to dig your own. A listing of rock shops would be too extensive to include in a book such as this. A good place to get information on rock shops in the area you plan to visit is to contact the chamber of commerce for that area. Rock shops may be able to provide information not only on rockhounding field trips but also on local rock clubs that sponsor trips.

Through mine tours you can see how minerals and gems were and are taken from the earth. On these tours, visitors learn what miners go through to remove the ores from the earth. This will give you a better appreciation for those sparkly gems you see in the showroom windows, and for many of the items we all take for granted in daily use.

You will meet other rockhounds at the mine. Attending one of the yearly events listed in the guide will also give you the chance to meet people who share your interest in gems and minerals and exchange ideas, stories, and knowledge of the hobby.

How to Use This Guide

To use this book, you can pick a state and determine what mining is available there, or pick a gem or mineral and determine where to go to "mine" it.

In this guide are indexes that will make the guide simple to use. If you are interested in finding a particular gem or mineral, go to the Index by Gem or Mineral in the back of the book. In this index, gems and minerals are listed in alphabetical order with the states and cities where fee dig sites for that gem or mineral may be found.

If you are interested in learning of sites near where you live, or in the area where you are planning a vacation, or if you simply want to know whether there are gems and minerals in a particular location, go to the Index by State, located in the back of the guide. The state index entries are broken down into three categories: Fee Dig Sites/Guide Services, Museums and Mine Tours, and Special Events and Tourist Information.

There are also several special indexes for use in finding your birthstone, anniversary stone, or zodiac stone.

Site Listings

The first section of each chapter lists fee dig sites and guide services that are available in each state. Included with the location of each site is a description of the site, directions to find it, what equipment is provided, and what you must supply. Costs are listed, along with specific policies of the site. Also included are other services available at the site and information on camping, lodging, etc. in the area of the site. Included in the section with fee dig sites are guide services for collecting gems and minerals.

In the second section of each chapter, museums of special interest to the gem/mineral collector and mine tours available to the public are listed. Besides being wonderful ways to learn about earth science, geology, and mining history (many museums and tours also offer child-friendly exhibits), museums are particularly useful for viewing gems and minerals in their rough or natural state before going out in the field to search for them.

The third section of each chapter lists special events involving gems and minerals, and resources for general tourist information.

A sample of the listings for fee dig mines and guide services (Section 1 in the guides) is on the next page.

Tips for mining:

1. Learn what gems or minerals can be found at the mine you are going to visit.
2. Know what the gem or mineral that you're hunting looks like in the rough before you begin mining.

Visiting local rock shops and museums will help in this effort.

3. When in doubt, save any stone that you are unsure about. Have an expert at the mine or at a local rock shop help you identify your find.

Sample Fee Dig Site Listing

TOWN in which the site is located / *Native or enriched[1]* • *Easy, moderate, difficult[2]*

Dig your own *T*

The following gems may be found:
- List of gems and minerals found at the mine

Mine name
Owner or contact (where available)
Address
Phone number
Fax
E-mail address
Website address

Open: months, hours, days
Info: Descriptive text regarding the site, including whether equipment is provided

Admission: Fee to dig; costs for predug dirt
Other services available
Other area attractions (at times)
Information on lodging or campground facilities (where available)
Directions

Map (where available)

Notes:

1. Native or enriched. *Native* refers to gems or minerals found in the ground at the site, put there by nature. *Enriched* means that gems and minerals from an outside source have been brought in and added to the soil. Enriching is also called "salting"—it is a guaranteed return. Whatever is added in a salted mine is generally the product of some commercial mine elsewhere. Thus, it is an opportunity to "find" gemstones from around the world the easy way, instead of traveling to jungles and climbing mountains in remote areas of the globe. Salted mines are particularly nice for giving children the opportunity to find a wide variety of gems and become involved in gem identification. The authors have tried to indicate if a mine is enriched, but to be sure, ask at the mine beforehand. If the status could not be determined, this designation was left out.

2. Sites are designated as easy, moderate, or difficult. This was done to give you a feel for what a site may be like. You should contact the site and make a determination for yourself if you have any doubts.

Easy: This might be a site where the gem hunter simply purchases bags or buckets of predug dirt, washes the ore in a flume or screens the gem-bearing gravel to concentrate the gems, and flips the screen. The gems or minerals are then picked out of the material remaining in the screen. A mine which has set aside a pile of mine material for people to pick through would be another type of site designated as "Easy."

Moderate: Mining at a "Moderate" site might mean digging with a shovel, then loading the dirt into buckets, followed by sifting and sluicing. Depending on your knowledge of mineral identification, work at a "Moderate" site might include searching the surface of the ground at an unsupervised area for a gem or mineral you are not familiar with (this could also be considered difficult).

Difficult: This might be a site requiring tools such as picks and shovels, or sledgehammers and chisels. The site may be out of the way and/or difficult to get to. Mining might involve heavy digging with the pick and shovel or breaking gems or minerals out of base rock using a sledge or chisel.

Special Note:

Although most museums and many fee dig sites are handicapped accessible, please check with the listing directly.

Maps

Maps are included to help you locate the sites in the guide. At the beginning of each state, there is a state map showing the general location of towns where sites are located.

Local maps are included in a listing when the information was available. *These maps are not drawn to scale!* These maps provide information to help you get to the site but are not intended to be a substitute for a road map. Please check directly with the site you are interested in for more detailed directions.

Fees

Fees listed in these guides were obtained when the book was updated, and may have changed. They are included to give you at least a general idea of the costs you will be dealing with. Please contact the site directly to confirm charges.

Many museums have discounts for members and for groups, as well as special programs for school groups. Please check directly with the institution for information. Many smaller and/or private institutions have no fee, but do appreciate donations to help meet the costs of staying open.

Many sites accept credit cards; some may not. Please check ahead for payment options if this is important.

Requesting Information by Mail

When requesting information by mail, it is always appreciated if you send a SASE (self-addressed stamped envelope) along with your request. Doing this will often speed up the return of information.

Equipment and Safety Precautions

Equipment

The individual sites listed in these guides often provide equipment at the mine. Please note that some fee dig sites place limitations on the equipment you can use at their site. Those limitations will be noted where the information was available. Always abide by the limitations; remember that you are a guest at the site.

On the following pages are figures showing equipment for rockhounding. Figures A and B identify some of the equipment you may be told you need at a site. Figure C shows material needed to collect, package, transport, and record your findings. Figure D illustrates typical safety equipment.

Always use safety glasses with side shields or goggles when you are hammering or chiseling. Chips of rock or metal from your tools can fly off at great speed in any direction when hammering. Use gloves to protect your hands as well.

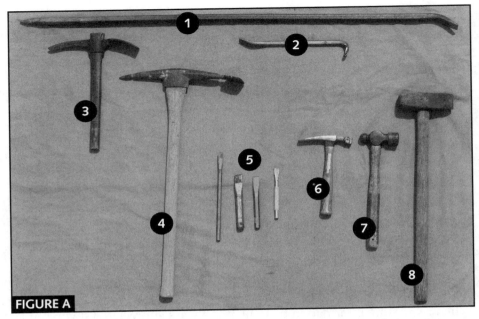

FIGURE A

1. Crowbar
2. Pry bar
3. Smaller pick
4. Rock pick
5. Various-sized chisels (*Note:* When working with a hammer and chisel, you may want to use a chisel holder, not shown, for protecting your hand if you miss. Always use eye protection with side shields and gloves!)
6. Rock hammer (*Note:* Always use eye protection.)
7. 3-pound hammer (*Note:* Always use eye protection.)
8. Sledgehammer (*Note:* When working with a sledgehammer, wear hard-toed boots along with eye protection.)

Other useful tools not shown include an ultraviolet hand lamp, and a hand magnifier.

Not pictured, but something you don't want to forget, is your camera and plenty of extra film. You may also want to bring along your video camera to record that "big" find, no matter what it might be.

Not pictured, but to be considered: knee pads and seat cushions.

Other Safety Precautions

- Never go into the field or on an unsupervised site alone. With protective clothing, reasonable care, proper use of equipment, and common sense,

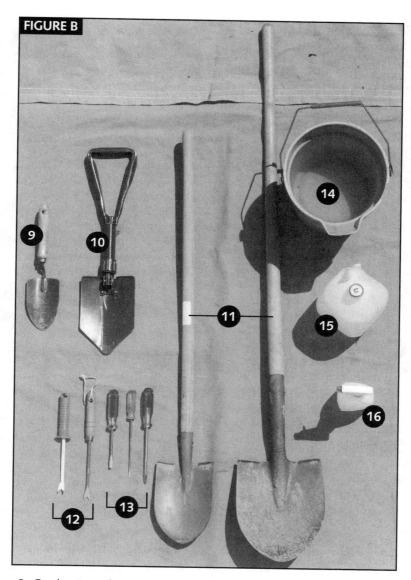

FIGURE B

9. Garden trowel
10. Camp shovel
11. Shovels
12. Garden cultivators
13. Screwdrivers

14. Bucket of water
15. (Plastic) jug of water
16. Squirt bottle of water; comes in handy at many of the mines to wash off rocks so you can see if they are or contain gem material

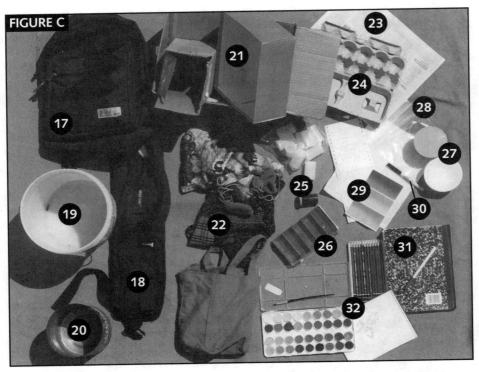

FIGURE C

17. Backpack
18. Waist pack to hold specimens
19. Bucket to hold specimens
20. Coffee can to hold specimens
21. Boxes to pack, transport, and ship specimens
22. Bags—various sized bags to carry collected specimens in the field
23. Newspaper to wrap specimens for transport
24. Egg cartons to transport delicate specimens
25. Empty film canisters to hold small specimens
26. Plastic box with dividers to hold small specimens
27. Margarine containers to hold small specimens

28. Reclosable plastic bags to hold small specimens
29. Gummed labels to label specimens (Whether you are at a fee dig site or with a guide, usually there will be someone to help you identify your find. It is a good idea to label the find when it is identified so that when you reach home, you won't have boxes of unknown rocks.)
30. Waterproof marker for labeling
31. Field log book to make notes on where specimens were found
32. Sketching pencils, sketchbook, paint to record your finds and the surrounding scenery

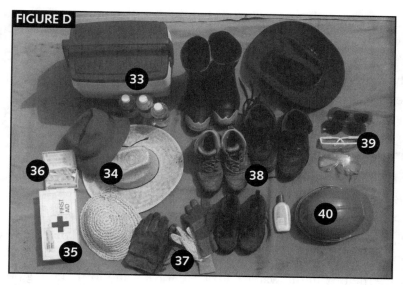

FIGURE D

33. Food and water—always carry plenty of drinking water (*Note:* many sites tell you in advance if they have food and water available or if you should bring some; however, it is always a good idea to bring extra drinking water. Remember—if you bring it in, pack it back out.)

34. Hats. Many of the sites are in the open, and the summer sun can be hot and dangerous to unprotected skin. Check with the site to see if they have any recommendations for protective clothing. Also, don't forget sunscreen.

35. First aid/safety kit

36. Snakebite kit. If the area is known to have snakes, be alert and take appropriate safety measures, such as boots and long pants. (*Note:* while planning our first gem-hunting trip, we read that the first aid kit should contain a snakebite kit. Just like rockhounds, snakes seem to love rocky areas!) In most cases, if you visit sites in the book, you will be either at a

flume provided by the facility, or with an experienced guide. At the first, you will most likely never see a snake; at the second, your guide will fill you in on precautions. For listings where you will be searching on a ranch or state park, ask about special safety concerns such as snakes and insects when you pay your fee. These sites may not be for everyone.

37. Gloves to protect your hands when you are working with sharp rock or using a hammer or chisel

38. Boots—particularly important at sites where you will be doing a lot of walking, or walking on rocks

39. Safety glasses with side shields, or goggles. Particularly important at hard rock sites or any site where you or others may be hitting rocks. Safety glasses are available with tinted lenses for protection from the sun.

40. Hard hats—may be mandatory if you are visiting an active quarry or mine; suggested near cliffs

accidents should be avoided, but in the event of an illness or accident, you always want to have someone with you who can administer first aid and call for or seek help.

- Always keep children under your supervision.
- Never enter old abandoned mines or underground diggings!
- Never break or hammer rocks close to another person!

Mining Techniques

How to Sluice for Gems

This is the most common technique used at fee dig mines where you buy a bucket of gem ore (gem dirt) and wash it at a flume.

1. Place a quantity of the gem ore in the screen box, and place the screen box in the water. Use enough gem ore to fill the box about a third.

2. Place the box in the water, and shake it back and forth, raising one side,

Clockwise from top: Gold pan; screen box used for sluicing; screen box used for screening.

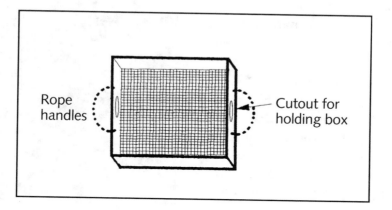

Rope handles

Cutout for holding box

How to Build a Screen Box

1. A screen box that is easy to handle is generally built from 1" x 4" lumber and window screening.

2. Decide on the dimensions of the screen box you want, and cut the wood accordingly. Dimensions generally run from 12" x 12" up to 18" x 18". Remember that the end pieces will overlap the side pieces, so cut the end pieces 1½" longer.

3. There are two alternative methods of construction. In one, drill pilot holes in the end pieces, and use wood screws to fasten the end pieces to the side pieces. In the other, use angle irons and screws to attach the ends and sides.

4. Cut the screening to be ¼" smaller than the outside dimensions of the screen box, and use staples to attach the screen to the bottom of the box. Use metal screening rather than plastic if possible. For a stronger box, cut ¼" or ⅜" hardware cloth to the same dimensions as the screening, and staple the hardware cloth over the screening. The hardware cloth will provide support for the screening.

5. Cut ¼" wood trim to fit, and attach it to the bottom of the box to cover the edges of the screening and hardware cloth and staples.

6. If you like, add rope handles or cut handholds in the side pieces for easier handling.

then the other, so that the material in the box moves back and forth. What you are doing is making the stones move around in the screen box, while washing dirt and sand out of the mixture.

3. After a minute or two of washing, take the screen box out of the flume, and let it drain. Look through the stones remaining in the screen box for your treasure. If you're not sure about something, ask one of the attendants.

4. When you can't finding anything more, put the box back in the flume and wash it some more, then take it out and search again.

5. If possible, move your screen box into bright light while you are searching, since the gems and minerals often show up better in bright light.

How to Screen for Gems

This is another common technique used at fee dig mines where you buy a bucket of gem ore and screen it for gems. (The authors used this technique for garnets and sapphires in Montana.)

1. Place a quantity of the gem ore in the screen box, and place the screen box in the water. Use enough gem dirt to fill the box about a third.

2. Place the box in the water, and begin tipping it back and forth, raising one side, then the other, so that the material in the box moves back and forth. What you are doing is making the gemstones, which are heavier than the rock and dirt, move into the bottom center of the screen box while at the same time washing dirt and sand out of the mixture.

3. After a minute or two, change the direction of movement to front and back.

4. Repeat these two movements (Steps 2 and 3) three or four times.

5. Take the box out of the water and let it drain, then place a board on top and carefully flip the box over onto the sorting table. It may be helpful to

put a foam pad in the box, then put the board over it. This helps keep the stones in place when you flip the box. If you have done it right, the gemstones will be found in the center of the rocks dumped onto the board. Use tweezers to pick the rough gemstones out of the rocks, and place them in a small container.

How to Pan for Gold

The technique for panning for gold is based on the fact that gold is much heavier than rock or soil. Gently washing and swirling the gold-bearing soil in a pan causes the gold to settle to the bottom of the pan. A gold pan has a flat bottom and gently slanting sides. Some modern pans also have small ridges or rings around the inside of the pan on these slanting sides. As the soil is washed out of the pan, the gold will slide down the sides, or be caught on the ridges and stay in the pan. Here's how:

1. Begin by filling the pan with ore, about ⅔ to ¾ full.

2. Put your pan in the water, let it gently fill with water, then put the pan under the water surface. Leave the pan in the water, and mix the dirt around in the pan, cleaning and removing any large rocks.

3. Lift the pan out of the water, then gently shake the pan from side to side while swirling it at the same time. Do this for 20–30 seconds to get the gold settled to the bottom of the pan.

4. Still holding the pan out of the water, continue these motions while tilting the pan so that the dirt begins to wash out. Keep the angle of the pan so that the crease (where the bottom and sides meet) is the lowest point.

5. When there is only about a tablespoon of material left in the pan, put about ½ inch of water in the pan, and swirl the water over the remaining material. As the top material is moved off, you should see gold underneath.

6. No luck? Try again at a different spot.

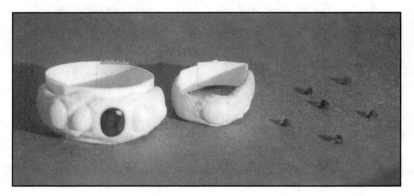

The authors sent their rough gems away for faceting. Using the faceted gems, they made crude mock-ups and sketches of the rings they wanted; then they sent the mock-ups, sketches, and gems to be made into rings.

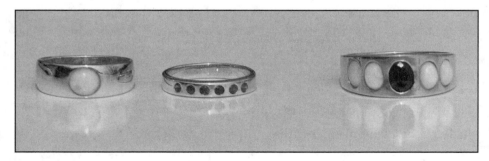

The finished rings.

Notes on Gem Faceting, Cabbing, and Mounting Services

Many of the fee dig sites offer services to cut and mount your finds. Quality and costs vary. Trade journals such as *Lapidary Journal* and *Rock & Gem* (available at most large bookstores or by subscription) list suppliers of these services, both in the United States and overseas. Again, quality and cost vary. Local rock and gem shops in your area may offer these services, or it may be possible to work with a local jeweler. Your local rock club may be able to provide these services or make recommendations.

After their first gem-hunting trip, the authors had some of their finds faceted and cabochoned. They then designed rings and had them made using these stones, as shown in the photos on the previous page.

Taking sifted gravel to the jig at a sapphire mine in Montana. Pictured from left to right: Steve, Kathy, Annie Rygle, Debra Pedersen, Kristen Pedersen.

ARIZONA

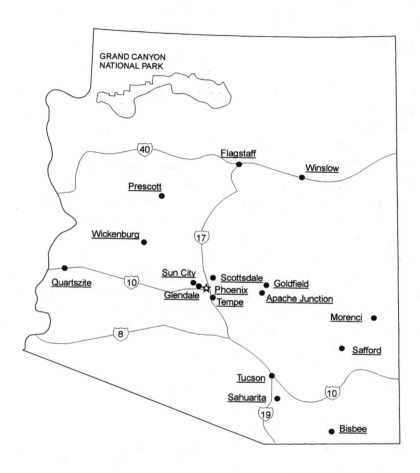

GRAND CANYON
NATIONAL PARK

40

Flagstaff

Winslow

Prescott

Wickenburg

17

Quartzsite

10

Sun City

Scottsdale

Goldfield

Glendale

Phoenix

Apache Junction

Tempe

Morenci

8

Safford

Tucson

Sahuarita

10

19

Bisbee

State Gemstone: Turquoise (1974)
State Mineral: Fire Agate
State Stone/Rock: Petrified Wood

APACHE JUNCTION / *Native ▪ Moderate*

Pan Your Own Gold *T*

The following gems or minerals may be found:

▪ Gold

Apache Trail Tours
P.O. Box 6146
Apache Junction, AZ 85278
Phone: (480) 982-7661
www.apachetrailtours.com

Open: Tours leave daily at 8:00 A.M. and 1:00 P.M.; closed Thanksgiving and Christmas. Tours do not run during the summer due to the heat.

Info: Apache Trail Tours runs two 4-hour gold panning jeep tours to the foothills of the Superstition Mountains. They will supply the pans and equipment. A metal detector is available for use.

Rates: $80.00 per person.

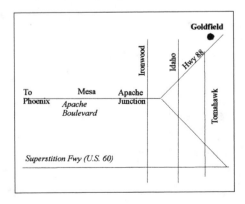

Other services available: The tours are based in Goldfield Ghost Town, which has stores, restaurants, and a museum.

Directions: Call for directions.

GLENDALE / *Native ▪ Moderate*

Guide Services, Collect Minerals *T*

The following gems or minerals may be found:

▪ Aragonite, fluorite, chrysocolla, quartz, galena, amethyst, fluorescent minerals, smithsonite, wulfenite in a variety of forms, willemite, calcite, barite.

Collection is at the following sites: Purple Passion Mine and Hogan Mine in Wickenburg, AZ; Spectrum Mine and Prism Mine in Aguila, AZ; and Amethyst Hill Claim.

William Gardner III
4608 W. Bluefield Avenue
Glendale, AZ 85308
Phone: (602) 547-2234

Open: By appointment.

Info: The Purple Passion Mine, originally called the Diamond Joe Mine, is known for good quality wulfenite, sometimes found in very odd crystal habits, such as acicular (needles), and needle growth on tabular crystals. The Hogan Mine yields similar material, but in different colors and forms. Galena, amethyst, and wulfenite can be found at the Prism Mine while the other minerals can be found at both the Prism and Spectrum mines. Upon request, Mr. Gardner will arrange a collecting trip to his Amethyst Hill claim, then to the Monarch Mine, ending at the Purple Passion Mine. The Amethyst Hill claim has amethyst, green fluorite, (often banded with the amethyst) and, rarely, cerrusite.

Note: Almost all of the material at the Purple Passion Mine is fluorescent, so collecting is best done in the early evening or at night. Black plastic is used for daytime collecting, but it is much harder, especially when hot.

Admission: $100.00 total minimum per day for 1–10 people; keep all that you find.

Other services available: Way2Cool UV lights are available for sale, for use in collecting the fluorescent minerals.

Directions: Call Mr. Gardner for directions.

GOLDFIELD / *Easy*

Pan for Gold *T*

The following gems or minerals may be found:

- Gold

Goldfield Ghost Town, Scenic Railroad, and Mine Tours
4650 N. Mammoth Mine Road

Goldfield, AZ 85219
Phone: (480) 983-0333
www.goldfieldghosttown.com

Open: Daily, 10:00 A.M.–5:00 P.M.

Info: In the gold panning area at this site, you can pan gold like the prospectors of days gone by. You get a pan with real gold in it, and learn how to shake the pan to make the gold settle to the bottom. You also get a vial for storing your gold flakes and small nuggets.

Panning Fee: $4.50/person. Group rates are available.

Other services available: See Section 2 for information on the mine tour and other attractions.

Directions: 3½ miles north of Apache Junction on Arizona Highway 88.

PRESCOTT / *Native • Moderate*

Pan for Gold *T*

The following gems or minerals may be found:

- Gold

Lynx Creek Mineral Withdrawal Area
Prescott National Forest
344 S. Cortez Street
Prescott, AZ 86303
Phone: (928) 443-8000
TTY: (928) 443-8001
http://www.fs.fed.us/r3/prescott

Open: All Prescott National Forest offices are open Monday–Friday, 8:00 A.M.–4:30 P.M. all year; closed major holidays.

Info: Pan for gold. No mechanized panning equipment is allowed. See the website or contact Prescott National Forest offices for important mining and recreational tips.

Admission: Small national park recreational and parking fee.

Other services available: Cabins and camping available in the national forest, as well as many recreational activities.

Directions: Prescott National Forest is comprised of 1.2 million acres; roughly ½ of the forest lies west of the city, and ½ to the east. Maps of the Lynx Creek Withdrawal Area are available from the website or the national forest offices.

SAFFORD / *Native · Moderate*

Hunt for Fire Agates *T*

The following gems or minerals may be found:

- **Fire agates**

Black Hills Rockhound Area
BLM Field Office
711 14th Avenue
Safford, AZ 85546
Phone: (928) 348-4400

Open: All year; however, summer may be too hot for enjoyable collecting. The BLM office is open Monday–Friday, 7:15 A.M.–4:45 P.M.; closed on major holidays.

Info: This undeveloped area is open for agate digging by the public without permits. Shovels and picks can be used to dig for fire agates. Most agate is found within the top 2 feet of the surfaces. Please backfill holes, as they pose a hazard to others. Agates can also be discovered on the surface near washes.

Admission: Free.

Other services available: Primitive camping is allowed for up to 2 weeks; no facilities.

Directions: Located on the north side of Arizona Route 191, about 18 miles north of Safford. Take U.S. Highway 70 east from Safford for 10 miles, then take U.S. Highway 191 north to a point just beyond milepost 141. You will see the entry sign on the left. Follow the dirt entry road for two miles to the sign at the center of the rockhound area.

Note: Please see the notes on "Rockhounding on BLM land" in Section 3 on Arizona.

Safety Note: Rattlesnakes may be found in certain areas during the warm months. Watch out for them in rock slides and around damp areas, in deep holes (where you can't see the bottom when you look in), and under old buildings and ledges.

SAFFORD / *Native · Moderate*

Hunt for Fire Agates *T*

The following gems or minerals may be found:

- **Mostly small pieces of fire agate, chalcedony, small geodes**

Round Mountain Rockhound Area
BLM Field Office
711 14th Avenue
Safford, AZ 85546
Phone: (928) 348-4400
www.arizonarocks.net

Open: All year; however, summer may be too hot for enjoyable collecting. The BLM office is open Monday–Friday, 7:15 A.M.– 4:45 P.M.; closed on major holidays.
Info: Hunt for fire agates in a BLM designated rockhounding area. The BLM office has maps and information available.
Admission: Free
Other services available: Primitive camping is allowed for up to 2 weeks; no facilities.
Directions: The site is located on a dirt road, 12 miles from a main highway. Although the site is located in Arizona, the dirt road starts out in New Mexico. From Highway 70 east of Safford approximately 50 miles, travel into New Mexico. Just beyond milepost 5, take the dirt access road on your right for 12 miles, following the signs to the rockhound area.
Note: Please see the notes on "Rockhounding on BLM land" in Section 3 on Arizona.
Safety Note: Rattlesnakes may be found in certain areas during the warm months. Watch out for them in rock slides and around damp areas, in deep holes (where you can't see the bottom when you look in), and under old buildings and ledges.

Dig for Gems and Minerals *T*
The following gems or minerals may be found:
▪ **Amethyst scepters, quartz, garnet, tourmaline, limonite**

Fat Jack Mine
Gary and Nancy Spraggins
1928 E. Colgate Drive
Tempe, AZ 85283
Phone: (480) 839-0151
E-mail: freebird@shakras.com

Open: April–October, depending on weather, by reservation only.
Info: The mine, located at 7,000 feet in the Bradshaw Mountains, was an old gold mine where the miners tossed the crystals that kept getting in the way of looking for gold. Today, these crystals are what people look for. Normally, you would meet at Crown King around 9:00 A.M., and drive to the mine entrance, then walk ½ mile up to the mine pit. (The last few hundred feet are fairly steep; assistance will be provided to people who might have difficulty making the climb.) Material from the mine is spread out around the pit for diggers to search. Bring small shovels, picks, rakes, screwdrivers, and screens to dig with. Keep all that you find.
Note: There is no water at the mine so bring fluids to drink, as well as your lunch. Also, bring protection from the sun.
Admission: $20.00 per person.

Other services available: Picnic tables for resting or eating, primitive camping at the mine entrance, no facilities. The mine is located in a national forest.

Directions: Directions will be provided when you make your reservation.

WICKENBURG / *Easy*

Pan for Gold

The following gems or minerals may be found:

▪ Gold

Robson's Mining World
P.O. Box 3465
Wickenburg, AZ 85358

Phone: (928) 685-2609
www.robsonminingworld.com

Open: October 1–May 1, Monday–Friday, 10:00 A.M.–4:00 P.M.; 9:00 A.M.–5:00 P.M., Saturday–Sunday.

Info: Learn how to pan for gold.

Admission: Adults (11–54) $5.00, seniors (55+) $4.50, children under 11 free.

Panning fee: None

Other services available: Bed & breakfast accommodations, restaurant, cowboy cookouts, display of mining equipment.

Directions: Highway 60 west from Wickenburg to Highway 71; turn right onto Highway 71 and drive 2 to 3 miles to Robson's Mining World.

SECTION 2: Museums and Mine Tours

APACHE JUNCTION

Museum 🏛

Superstition Mountain Museum
4087 N. Apache Trail
Apache Junction, AZ 85219
Phone: (480) 983-4888
E-mail: smhsgold@aol.com
www.superstitionmountainmuseum.org

Open: Daily, 9:00 A.M.–3:00 P.M. Closed Thanksgiving and four Chrsitmas days.

Info: The museum contains exhibits on geology, minerals, maps, mining, and history of the area.

Admission: Adults $4.00 (18–54), seniors (55+) $3.00, students 6–17 $2.00, under 5 free.

Other attractions: Nearby Apache Junction is the home of the Superstitions, the legendary Lost Dutchman Gold Mine, the Lost Dutchman Monument, and the Apache Trail. Recreation includes hiking and horseback riding. See Lost Dutchman State Park and Roosevelt Dam, cruise the lakes, or visit an Old West-style mining camp.

Directions: Four miles northeast of Apache Junction on the Apache Trail (State Highway 88).

BISBEE

Mine Tour

Queen Mine Tours
Dart Road
Bisbee, AZ 85603
Phone (Mine): (886) 432-2071 or
(Visitor Center) (520) 432-2071
www.cityofbisbee.com/queenminetours

Open: Queen Mine underground tours: 7 days/week, 9:00, 10:30 A.M., noon, 2:00 P.M., 3:30 P.M.

Van tour of surface mine: 7 days/week, 10:30 A.M., noon, 2:00 P.M., 3:30 P.M.

Info: The first mining claim was filed in Bisbee in 1877, and mining began in 1880. Bisbee was a center for copper mining, along with gold, silver, lead, and zinc. Mining ended in the mid-1970s. Over 300 distinct mineral species have been identified from the copper mine at Bisbee. Specimens from Bisbee are in numerous museum collections, including all the Arizona museums listed here.

The Queen Mine underground tour is conducted by former miners. Jackets and walking shoes are recommended, as it is 47°F in the mine. A van tour of the surface mine and the historic district is also available. All tours leave from the Queen Mine Tour Building located immediately south of Old Bisbee's Business District off the U.S. 80 interchange.

Fees: (taxes added to all fees)
▪ Underground mine tours: Adults $12.00 + tax, youth (4–15) $5.50 + tax, children under 4 years free.
▪ Van tours: $10.00 + tax/person, under 3 years free. Reservations suggested.
▪ Other attractions: Bisbee Mining and Historical Museum, a Smithsonian Institute Affiliate (open 10:00 A.M.– 4:00 P.M. daily).

Directions: Take old historic Bisbee interchange off U.S. 80.

FLAGSTAFF

Geologic Landmark

Meteor Crater Enterprises, Inc.
P.O. Box 30940
Flagstaff, AZ 86003-0940
Phone: (800) 289-5898
E-mail: info@meteorcrater.com
www.meteorcrater.com

Open: All year, daily, Memorial Day–Labor Day, 7:00 A.M.–7:00 P.M.; rest of the year, 8:00 A.M.–5:00 P.M.; closed Christmas Day.

Info: Meteor Crater is a gaping chasm 550 feet deep, nearly a mile across, and over 2.4 miles in circumference. It was formed by meteorite impact 50,000 years ago. The topographical terrain of Meteor Crater so closely resembles that of earth's moon and other planets that NASA designated it one of the official training sites for the Apollo astronauts.

View the crater from observation decks overhanging its depths. Meteor Crater is the best-preserved meteorite impact site on earth and has been designated a National Landmark. Walking tours are available at no extra charge between 9:15 A.M. and 2:15 P.M. Tours leave hourly, weather permitting.

Meteor Crater's Museum offers interactive displays of theater shows. Also, a 1,406-lb. meteorite is on display.

Astronaut Park, which is dedicated to crew members of the Apollo I, Challenger and Columbia spacecrafts, provides a place to picnic or just relax. Also, the Astronaut Hall of Fame lists the names of all American astronauts. An Apollo Space Capsule is on display.

Admission: Adults $12.00, seniors $11.00, children (6–17) $6.00, under 5 free.

Other services available: Gift store and lapidary shop, sandwich shop and restaurant, RV park.

Directions: Easily accessible from I-40, 35 miles east of Flagstaff or 20 miles west of Winslow.

FLAGSTAFF

Museum

Museum of Northern Arizona
3101 N. Ft. Valley Road
Flagstaff, AZ 86001
Phone: (928) 774-5213
Fax: (928) 779-1527

Open: Daily, 9:00 A.M.–4:00 P.M.; closed major holidays.

Info: Presents the history of the Colorado Plateau, including geologic models and mineral specimens.

Admission: Adults $5.00, seniors $4.00, students $3.00, children (7–17) $2.00.

Directions: On Highway 180, three miles north of Flagstaff.

GOLDFIELD

Mine Tour

Goldfield Ghost Town, Scenic Railroad, and Mine Tours
4650 N. Mammoth Mine Road
Goldfield, AZ 85219
Phone: (480) 983-0333
www.goldfieldghosttown.com

Open: Daily, 10:00 A.M.–5:00 P.M.

Info: The Goldfield Mining District was founded in 1892, when a rich gold strike was made at the base of the Superstition Mountains. Millions of dollars worth of gold ore was removed over the next 5 years.

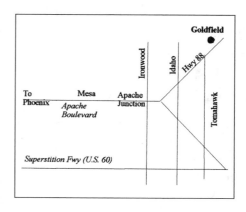

Features: Dynamite mine tours, gold panning, museum, antique mining equipment, train rides, horseback riding, and more.

Admission: Free admission into town. Mine tour: Adults $6.00, seniors (55+) $5.00, children (6–12) $3.00, under 5 free. Train ride: Adults $5.00, seniors $4.00, children (5–12) $3.00, under 4 free. Group rates are available.

Other services available: Ride a narrow-gauge railroad (Arizona's only working narrow-gauge railroad); rock shop; gift shop; gourmet shop; bakery; steak house and 1890s saloon. Train runs Thursday–Sunday, June–September.

Directions: 3½ miles north of Apache Junction on Arizona Highway 88.

MORENCI

Mine Tour 🏛

Phelps Dodge Morenci Copper Mine
Morenci, AZ 85540
Phone: (877) 646-8687

Open: Tours offered Friday and Saturday at 8:30 A.M. and 1:00 P.M.

Info: Take a 2½ hour tour of one of America's scenic and industrial wonders. Tours are by reservation only, and start at the Morenci Motel. After an orientation, buses take you through the operations at one of America's largest open-pit mines.

Fees: Adults $8.00, seniors (65+) $6.00, youth 9–17 $4.00, children under 9 are not permitted on tour due to safety regulations.

Other services available: Gift shop, restaurant.

Directions: Located in Greenlee County, in eastern Arizona. Get specific directions when making reservations.

PHOENIX

Museum 🏛

Arizona Mining and Mineral Museum
1502 West Washington
Phoenix, AZ 85007
Phone: (602) 255-3791

Open: All year, 8:00 A.M.–5:00 P.M. Monday–Friday; 11:00 A.M.– 4:00 P.M. Saturday. **Library:** 8:00 A.M.–5:00 P.M. Monday–Friday.

Info: Over 3,000 minerals are on exhibit. Included are many minerals from Arizona's copper mines, a chunk of Meteor Crater's meteorite, rocks from the original landing on the moon, a case of spheres, a fluorescent display, and the collection of the Arizona Mineral and Mining Museum Foundation. Outside exhibits of mining equipment include

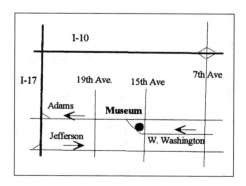

reconstructions of the Boras Headframe moved from Bisbee, AZ, 1882 baby-gauge steam railroad locomotive No. 2 from Phelps Dodge-Morenci, a mucker car, and an ore car. Plans are underway to add a 19-foot-tall four-stamp mill.

Admission: $2.00.

Other services available: Gift shop with large area dedicated to Arizona minerals. Lapidary shop, which provides training for those interested in rock-hounding and lapidary art. The museum is part of the Department of Mines and Mineral Resources, which houses 10,000 files on mines and mineral occurrences in Arizona, plus a library. Both are open to the public.

Directions: From the east or west: use I-10, exit at 7th Avenue, go south on 7th Avenue to Washington, then turn west to 15th Avenue.

From the north: take I-17 to the Jefferson exit (the first exit south of the I-10/I-17 stack), then turn east on Jefferson to 15th Avenue, then travel 1 block north to Washington.

From the south: take I-17 to the Adams/Van Buren exit, and turn east on Van Buren to 15th Avenue, then turn south for 3 blocks to Washington.

ADMMR is on the NW corner of Washington and 15th Avenue. Free parking is available to the north and east of the building.

SAHUARITA

Museum

ASARCO Mineral Discovery Center
1421 W. Pima Mine Road
Sahuarita, AZ 85629

Enjoy views of open-pit mines at these outlooks in the Tucson area.

New Cornelia Open-pit Mine

Arizona's largest open-pit mine is 1½ miles across. From Tucson, take State Highway 86 west for 130 miles to Ajo, then turn southwest on La Mina Avenue, then southwest on Indian Village Road, and follow the signs to the outlook.

Ray Mine

This open-pit mine is located 85 miles north of Tucson and can be reached by driving on State Highway 77 to Winkleman; then take State Highway 177 north for 20 miles, past Kelvin to the overlook.

Phone: (520) 625-7513
E-mail: amdcinfo@asarco.com
www.mineraldiscovery.com

Open: Tuesday–Saturday, 9:00 A.M.–5:00 P.M. Contact for tour schedule.

Info: The center features exhibits on geology, mining, and the use of minerals. It also has displays of historic and modern mining equipment. Mineral displays of drusy chrysacolla, native copper, malachite, Peruvian pyrite, zincite, fluorite, rhodochrosite, and other copper bearing minerals are situated throughout the visitor's center.

Tours of the ASARCO Mission open-pit mine and mill facilities are available.

Admission to center: Free.

Tours: Adults $6.00, seniors $5.00, children (5–12) $4.00. Group discounts are available; call (520) 625-7513, option 2.

Other services available: Gift shop.

Directions: Twenty minutes south of Tucson. Take I-19 south to exit 80. The entrance to the center is 300 feet from the exit.

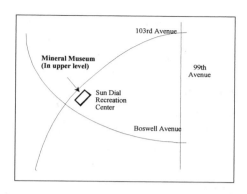

P.M., Monday–Wednesday, and Friday, October–April. Closed July and August.

Info: Over 2,000 rocks and minerals from across the country and around the world are on exhibit, with an emphasis on minerals from Arizona. Exhibits include lapidary and fossil displays, and a display of over 150 fluorescent rocks responding to ultraviolet light from both long- and short-wave lamps. Many of the specimens in this exhibit are from Franklin and Sterling Hill Mines, Sussex County, N.J.

Admission: Free; donations accepted.

Directions: Located on the upper level of the Sun Dial Recreation Center at the corner of 103rd Street and Boswell Boulevard.

SUN CITY

Museum 🏛

The Mineral Museum
Sun City Rockhound Club
14801 103rd Avenue, Upper Level
Sun City, AZ 85351
Does not have phone

Open: 9:00 A.M.–noon, Tuesday–Friday, June and September; 10:00 A.M.–3:00

TEMPE

Museum 🏛

Robert S. Dietz Museum of Geology
Physical Sciences Complex, F-Wing
Arizona State University
Tempe, AZ 85287
Phone: (480) 965-7065
E-mail: barcher@asu.edu

Open: 9:00 A.M.–Noon, Monday–Friday.

Info: Mineral displays, particularly relating to Arizona minerals; seismograph.

Admission: Free

Directions: On the Arizona State University campus, in ASU's Physical Sciences Complex F-Wing

TUCSON

Museum

Arizona-Sonora Desert Museum
2021 N. Kinney Road
Tucson, AZ 85743-2702
Phone: (520) 883-1380
E-mail: info@desertmuseum.org
www.desertmuseum.org/index.html

Open: Every day of the year; 7:30 A.M.–5:00 P.M., March–September; 8:30 A.M.–5:00 P.M., October–February; open Saturday nights until 10:00 P.M., June–August.

Info: The focus of the Desert Museum's Permanent Mineral Collection is on the Sonoran Desert region of Arizona, Sonora, and Baja California. There are nearly 4,000 known mineral species. The Sonora Desert region has at least 1,500, or almost 38%, of all known minerals. The Permanent Mineral Collection at the Desert Museum contains about half of the mineral species known to be in the region. The philosophy behind the Desert Museum's exhibits is to "dazzle its guests with the beauty of the mineral kingdom, instill an appreciation for these natural works of art, and initiate an awareness of the need to preserve them."

Admission: Adults $9.00, children (6–12) $2.00, children under 6 free, May–October. Adults $12.00, children $4.00 November–April. Group discounts are available.

Other services available: Gift shop.

Directions: The museum is located in Tucson Mountain Park, 14 miles west of Downtown Tucson. From I-19, take State Highway 86 West (Exit 99) to Kinney Road. Turn right on Kinney Road to the Museum. From I-10, take West Speedway Boulevard (Exit 257) up through Gates Pass to Kinney Road. Turn right on Kinney Road to the museum on your left. (*Note: Gates Pass is unsuited to RVs and trailers.*)

TUCSON

Museum

Flandrau Science Center
1601 East University Blvd.
Tucson, AZ 85719
Phone: (520) 621-7827
www.flandrau.org

Special note: Flandrau's exhibit halls and planetarium are closed for renovations until August 31, 2006. The University of Arizona Mineral Museum (lower level of the Science Center) may be open by appointment. Call (520) 621-4227.

The new "Miner's Story Project" will preserve and share stories about life in mines and mining communities in the southeast United States.

Open: All year, 9:00 A.M.–5:00 P.M. Tuesday–Sunday.

Info: About 2,100 of the 15,000 specimens in the university collection are on view. Exhibits include Arizona and Mexico wulfenite, Bisbee malachites, and azurite, large tri-state fluorite and galena specimens, vivid uranium minerals from the Colorado plateau, a selection of the Mammoth-St. Anthony mine minerals, Mexican minerals, a small collection of meteorites, well-crystalized borate minerals from California, and fluorescent minerals.

Also on exhibit is a selection of about 400 rough and cut gems showing the beauty of gemmy varieties of some of the common (and less expensive) minerals. Large mineral specimens are set about the room so they can be touched by children and adults.

Admission: Call for prices when reopened.

Directions: Located on the campus of the University of Arizona, at the corner of Cherry Avenue and University Boulevard. Take Speedway Boulevard (Exit 257) from I-10 East to Campbell Avenue. Turn right onto Campbell Avenue and drive ½ mile to Enke Drive, and turn right. Drive to the end of the road and turn right on Cherry. Parking lot is at corner of Cherry and University.

WICKENBURG

Old Mining Village Tour/ Mining Equipment Display

Robson's Mining World
P.O. Box 3465
Wickenburg, AZ 85358
Phone: (928) 685-2609
www.robsonminingworld.com

Open: 10:00 A.M.–4:00 P.M., Monday–Friday, October 1–May 1; Saturday–Sunday, 9:00 A.M.–5:00 P.M.

Info: Reconstruction of the Nell-Meda gold mining camp, with old mining equipment on display.

Admission: Adults (11–54) $5.00, seniors $4.50, children under 11 free.

Other services available: Bed & breakfast accommodations, restaurant, cowboy cookouts.

Directions: Highway 60 west from Wickenburg to Highway 71; turn right onto Highway 71 and drive 2 to 3 miles to Robson's Mining World.

WICKENBURG

Mine Tour

Vulture Gold Mine
John & Marge Osborne
36610 N. 335 Avenue
Wickenburg, AZ 85390
Phone: (602) 859-2743

Open: 8:00 A.M.–4:00 P.M., Thursday–Monday, fall and winter; 8:00 A.M.–4:00 P.M., Friday–Sunday, spring and summer. **Info:** Open for self-guided tours. The Vulture Gold Mine was the most productive gold mine in the history of Arizona. It was closed during WW II, and never reopened.

Note: The mine is currently for sale; new owners may change times and fees. Call before going to the mine.

Admission: Adults $5.00, children 6–12 $4.00. Not recommended for children under six.

Directions: Route U.S. 60 from Phoenix leads to Wickenburg. The Vulture Gold Mine is located 12 miles southwest of Wickenburg, on Vulture Mine Road, which joins U.S. 60 west of Wickenburg.

SECTION 3: Special Events and Tourist Information

ANNUAL EVENT

Minerals of Arizona ☞

Held for one day in March/April, this symposium discusses minerals in Arizona and Mexico and presents information on gem and mineral collecting.

Sponsored by the Arizona Mineral and Mining Museum Foundation and the Arizona Department of Mines and Mineral Resources.

For more information:
Arizona Mineral and Mining Museum Foundation
www.azminfun.com

ANNUAL EVENT

Quartzsite Gem and Mineral Shows/Sales, Quartzsite, AZ ☞

In January and February, there are eight different gem and mineral shows in Quartzsite.

For more information:
Quartzsite Chamber of Commerce
495 Main Event Lane
Quartzsite, AZ 85346
Phone: (928) 927-5600
www.quartzsitechamber.com

ANNUAL EVENT

Tucson Gem and Mineral Shows, Tucson, AZ

From the end of January through the middle of February, more than 25 gem and mineral shows are held by a wide variety of sponsoring organizations in Tucson. Originating from a show held in 1955 by the Tucson Gem and Mineral Society, this yearly event is now considered to be the world's largest gem and mineral show.

For more information:
www.tucsonshowguide.com
www.tgms.org

TOURIST INFORMATION

State Tourist Agency

Arizona Office of Tourism
1110 W. Washington, Suite 155
Phoenix, AZ 85007
Phone: (866) 275-5816
www.arizonaguide.com

Arizona rockhound and tourist information:
www.admmr.state.az.us/rockhound.htm

Rockhounding on BLM Land

"Rockhounding in Arizona" is a brochure produced by the Bureau of Land Management. It summarizes the regulations for rockhounding on public lands. The brochure is available from any BLM office in Arizona, including the Arizona State Office at 1 N. Central Avenue, Phoenix, AZ 85004 (Phone: [602] 417-9200). Briefly summarized, the regulations state that "you may collect reasonable amounts of specimens." In Arizona, the BLM sets the "'reasonable' limit for personal use as up to 25 pounds per day, plus one piece, with a total limit of 250 pounds per year."

CALIFORNIA

Yreka

5

101

Quincy

Nevada City Sierra City
Grass Valley Alleghany

Luceme

80 Coloma

Lakeport

Sacramento Placerville

Pine Grove
Jackson
Columbia Angels Camp
Sonora
San Francisco
580 Jamestown
680 Mariposa

YOSEMITE
NATIONAL
PARK

Pacific
Grove

Death
Valley

101

Independence

5

DEATH VALLEY
NATIONAL
MONUMENT

Shoshone

Paso Robles

Ridgecrest

Yermo
Boron 15

Santa
Barbara

40 Needles

101 Los Angeles Redlands Yucca
Valley

Avalon Riverside
Rancho Pala
Palos Verdes 10 Palo
Fallbrook Mesa Grande Verde

Julian
San Diego El Cajon 8

State Gemstone: Benitoite
State Mineral: Gold
State Stone/Rock: Serpentine

COLOMA / *Native • Moderate*

Pan for Gold *T*

The following gems or minerals may be found:

- Gold

Marshall Gold Discovery State Historic Park
P.O. Box 265
310 Back Street
Coloma, CA 95613
Phone: (530) 622-3470 (Park);
(530) 622-1116 (Museum)

Open: Park open daily, 8:00 A.M.–sunset. Museum open every day except Christmas and New Year's Day, 10:00 A.M.– 4:30 P.M.

Info: Pan for gold at the site where James Marshall first discovered and started the California Gold Rush of 1849.

The American River is a foothill river that washes gold particles down from the slowly eroding rock of the "mother lode." This placer gold collects in holes and sandbars along the river. The gold-panning area is located on the east side of the south fork of the American River next to the Pleasant Flat area and is accessible by crossing the Mt. Murphy bridge. Parking is available. Dogs are not allowed in the Pleasant Flat or gold-panning areas.

Admission: $5.00/car into the park.

Other services available: Museum, picnic area, restrooms.

For information on the Marshall Gold Discovery State Historic Park, see the listing under Section 2.

Directions: From Highway 49 (Main Street in Coloma), take Mt. Murphy Road across the American River. The gold panning area is just across the river from the park.

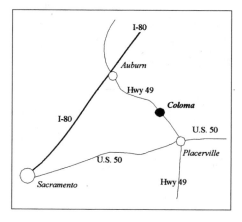

COLUMBIA / *Native · Easy*

Pan for Gold T

The following gems or minerals may be found:

- Gold, garnets

Hidden Treasure Gold Mine Tours
Matelot Gulch Mining Co., Inc.
P.O. Box 28
Columbia State Park, CA 95310
Phone: (209) 532-9693 or
(209) 533-3105

Open: All year; weather permitting. Winter days and hours vary, please call.

Info: In the Columbia State Historic Park, learn how to pan for gold at the Matelot Gulch Mining Co. Columbia State Historic Park is a restored Gold Rush boom town. Lessons in gold panning and a tour of an active gold mine are available. See listing in Section 2 for details on the mine tour.

Rates: Pan all day. Panning fee: $5.00 for panning lessons and guarantee to find gold in the first pan, $10.00 for panning lessons and guarantee to find gold and garnets, $3.00 for panning only. Group rates available.

Other services available: Horseback riding, stagecoach rides, restrooms, shops, restaurants.

Directions: On Parrotts Ferry Road, just north of Sonora on State Highway 49 or just east of Angels Camp on State Highway 4. Follow signs. The mining company office is located at the corner of Main and Washington Streets within Columbia State Historic Park.

JACKSON / *Native · Easy*

Pan for Gold T

The following gems or minerals may be found:

- Gold

Kennedy Gold Mine
P.O. Box 684
Jackson, CA 95642-0684
Phone: (209) 223-9542
kmmine@volcano.net
www.kennedygoldmine.com

Open: Mid-March–October 31, weekends only.

Info: The Kennedy Mine was started in the 1850s and was the deepest gold mine in North America when it was closed in 1942. Visitors can see the 125-foot head frame, tour several mine buildings, and try gold panning in the

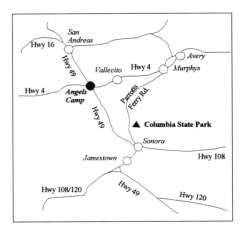

Kennedy Mine troughs. For information on the Kennedy Gold Mine Tour, see the listing under Section 2.

Admission: Adults $9.00, children (4–12) $5.00. Group tours with reservations.

Directions: Jackson is located at the intersection of State Highway 49 and State Highway 88.

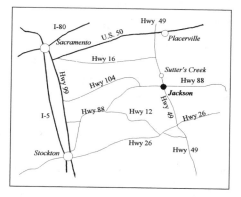

JAMESTOWN

Pan for Gold *T*

The following gems or minerals may be found:

- Gold

Gold Prospecting Adventures, LLC
18170 Main Street
P.O. Box 1040
Jamestown, CA 95327–1040
Phone: (209) 984-4653 or
(800) 596-0009
www.goldprospecting.com

Open: All year, 10:00 A.M.–3:00 P.M. Alternate times may be arranged by calling.

Info and Rates: Offers a variety of gold panning activities. Pan for gold at the Jimtown 1849 Gold Mining Camp for times ranging from 2 hours ($30.00 for an individual, $60.00 for a family of 5) to 5 hours (call for prices). Sluice and pan for gold for times ranging from 2 hours ($55.00–$85.00) to 2 days ($135.00–$265.00). The 2-day option includes use of a suction gun and hand-held viewer to look for nuggets. Metal detector instructions for looking for nuggets are available at $195.00 for 4 hours and $210.00 for 5 hours with an instructor. Highbanking trips are also available.

There are also three gold mining/prospecting courses offered: one on placer mining, one on electronic/pocket hunting, and one on mining claims. Contact Gold Prospecting Adventures for more information and costs. Group rates are also available.

Other services available: The 1849 Gold Mining Camp is an exact replica of the original camp, and has characters in period dress re-creating activities of the time (prospecting, panning, brawling, etc.). The camp has over 25 attractions.

Directions: Call for specific directions.

Find Your Own

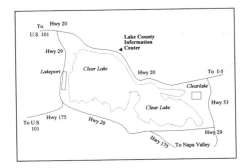

The following gems or minerals may be found:

- Quartz crystals (Lake County "Diamonds" or "Moon Tears")

Lake County Visitor Information
Center
6110 E. Highway 20
Lucerne, CA 95458
Phone: (707) 274-5652; (800) 525-3743
Fax: (707) 274-5664
E-mail: info@lakecounty.com
www.lakecounty.com

Info: Lake County "diamonds" were formed when silica contained in basalt carried by eruptions of Mt. Konocti (an old volcano overlooking the south shore of Clear Lake) was subjected to great pressure and crystallized. Subsequent geological shifting fractured it into fragments found today. Compared with most other quartz, these crystals are cleaner, purer, and harder. When these crystals are faceted, they resemble diamonds.

There are no fee dig sites for Lake County "diamonds," but rock shops around Clear Lake display and sell these stones, and some can facet them. They will also show you how to recognize them in the field. They may also tell you where you can find some yourself. Rockhounding is said to be best in the spring or fall months when light rains have exposed the crystals.

For other information on Quartz "Diamonds," see entries on Herkimer "Diamonds" and Cape May "Diamonds" (both in Vol. 4).

Moon Tears—The Legend of the Lake County "Diamond"

Long ago there were no stars in the sky; there was only the Moon and her brother the Sun. The Moon gave the people light in the darkness, and the Sun gave them light in the day. The Moon was gentle and kind, but the Sun was cruel and jealous of his beautiful sister.

In those days, there was a young Pomo chieftain who fell in love with the Moon. Night after night he would stand and sing to her as she crossed the sky. In the day he slept, and would not help his father fish, or hunt, or even mend the nets. His family was very concerned, for what he was doing was not right, and they also feared that the Sun might become angry and do something to harm all the people.

The Sun did become angry and sent Blue-Jay to lead the young man high into the mountains to where the Sun had a special place. It was a terrifying land. Great jets of steam came from the ground, and the streams were so hot no fish could swim in them. When the young man reached the place of the Sun, he fell into a deep sleep and could move no more.

That night the Moon saw the young chieftain sleeping and fell in love with him. She came and sang beside him, and the words of her song filled the air with many tiny golden pieces of dust. The Sun, her brother, came and ordered her away, saying, "You are needed by the People. Go back into the sky." The Moon knew her brother was right, but she was very sad and wept bitterly, and her tears caused the golden moondust to turn into bright pieces of clear crystal that fell to the ground. They became the Lake County "diamonds."

This made the Sun even angrier, and he decided to kill the young man. When the Moon saw this, she seized up handfuls of the bright tears and hurled them at her brother. Many of them stuck in the sky and became the stars. Those that fell back to earth are the Lake County "diamonds" that have a blue or lavender tinge. Then the Moon took the young chieftain to live with her in the sky. On clear nights, when the moon is full, if you look closely, you can see his face.

Another local Pomo Indian legend tells the story of the stone's origin as follows: When Indian chieftain Kah-Bel climbed the slopes of Mt. Konocte to visit the gravesite of his beloved daughter Princess Lupi-yana, he wept. His tears crystallized and rolled down the slopes of Mt. Konocte to the plains below.

Lake County "diamonds" were placed on burial mounds by some tribes to protect the spirits of the newly departed from evil spirits or demons, who loved the darkness and, when they saw the "moon tears," would think the moon was shining and go away.

It is said that these legends have come down to us through the ages, recited from generation to generation by the elders, who would gather around the campfire in the evening and listen to the ancient one tell of the "moon tears."

(These stories were provided by, and are reprinted with permission from, the Lake County Visitors Information Center.)

MARIPOSA / *Moderate*

Pan for Gold *T*

The following gems or minerals may be found:

- Gold

Little Valley Inn at the Creek
3483 Brooks Road
Mariposa, CA 95338
Phone: (209) 742-6204; (800) 889-5444
www.littlevalley.com

Open: All year, daily.
Info: Customers of the Little Valley Inn can pan for gold at the seasonal creek out back.
Rates: $104.00/double occupancy, includes breakfast; $150.00 suite; $130.00 cabin; ask about winter rates.

Other services available: Mariposa is located near Yosemite National Park.
Directions: Mariposa is located at the intersection of State Highway 140 (which goes between Merced and Yosemite) and State Highway 49.

MESA GRANDE / *Native • Moderate*

Dig for Tourmaline *T*

*The following gems or minerals
may be found:*

- **Tourmaline**

Himalayan Tourmaline Mine
High Desert Gems & Minerals
Phone: (775) 772-7724 (Phone some-
times not in network, so keep trying.)
E-mail: tourmalineminer@aol.com
www.highdesertgemsandminerals.com

Open: All year, by reservation only.
Info: Look for California tourmaline in
the mine tailings at the famous
Himalayan Tourmaline mine.
Fees: $50.00 per person.
Directions: Get directions when you
make your reservation.

NEVADA CITY / *Native • Moderate*

Pan for Gold *T*

*The following gems or minerals
may be found:*

- **Gold**

Malakoff Diggins Park Association
Malakoff Diggins State Historical Park
23579 N. Bloomfield Road
Nevada City, CA 95959
Phone: (530) 265-2740
www.parks.ca.gov

Park open: All year, daily. Call prior to
arrival, conditions may change.

Museum: Memorial Day–Labor Day,
daily 10:00 A.M.–4:30 P.M.; open weekends only in spring and fall.
Info: Malakoff Diggins State Historical
Park tells the story of the "free-for-all"
hydraulic gold mining era in California.
During the summer, rangers conduct gold
panning tours on weekends and town tours
daily. See the listing in Section 2 for information on the museum and other tours.
Admission: $6.00/developed parking.
Other services available: Family camping; group camping; cabins; fishing; hiking; swimming.

Directions: From Nevada City, travel 11
miles north on Highway 49 toward
Downieville. Turn right onto Tyler Foote
Road, stay on the pavement and follow
the yellow line to the park. The road
changes names a few times (Curzon
Grade Road, Back Bone Road, Derbec
Road, North Bloomfield Road). These
are not high speed roads. The park is 26
miles from Nevada City.

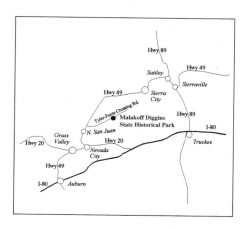

Collect Gems and Minerals

The following gems or minerals may be found:

- Pink, green, and bicolor tourmaline; garnets; book mica; smokey crystals; cleavelandite; kunzite; morganite; hiddenite; gossanite (clear beryl); purple lepidolite; muscovite; aquamarine

Oceanview Mine
c/o Stephen's Custom Jewelry
132 W. Grand Avenue
Escondido, CA 92025
Phone: (760) 489-1566 or
(760) 803-3428
www.digforgems.com

Open: All year, Sundays 11:00 A.M. –3:00 P.M. Reservations required.

Info: Material is blasted and hauled out of the mine for digging. Bring gloves, hat, lunch, water to drink, good walking shoes, and container or backpack to bring your treasures home. Tools are provided.

Rates: $50.00 per person; $185.00 per family 4 pack.

Other services available: Picnic tables, misters for hot weather, toilet facilities. A tour of the mine can be arranged during the lunch break.

Directions: You can get directions when you make your reservation. The group meets at the southwest end of the Pala Casino parking lot at 10:45 Sunday mornings to complete liability forms and finalize arrangements.

Pan for Gold

The following gems or minerals may be found:

- Gold, also quartz crystals, jade, jasper, and river rubies

Roaring Camp Mining Company
P.O. Box 278
Pine Grove, CA 95665
Phone: (209) 296-4100
E-mail: roaringcamp@volcano.net
www.volcano.net/~pineacre

Open: Daily from May–September. Daily guided gold panning tours leave at 10:00 A.M. and 2:30 P.M.

Info: A guided 4-hour tour takes visitors to Roaring Camp, an old 49er gold camp.

One week each month, a "Company Operations" is held, where a limited-number group uses the Roaring Camp mining equipment and all gold recovered is split evenly.

Rates: Call for current rates.

Other services available: Overnight camping in prospectors' camp cabins; Sat-

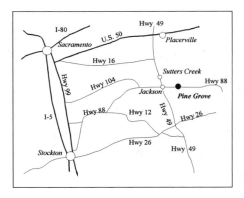

urday night barbecue dinner; swimming; "trading post"; snack shop.

Directions: Pine Grove is east from Jackson on Route 88.

PLACERVILLE / *Native · Easy*

Pan for Gold

The following gems or minerals may be found:

- **Gold (learn the art of gold panning)**

Hangtown's Gold Bug Park & Mine
2635 Gold Bug Lane
Placerville, CA 95667
Phone: (530) 642-5207
Guided Group Tours Line: (503) 642-5238
www.goldbugpark.org

Open: Park grounds open daily 8:30 A.M.–5:00 P.M. all year weather permitting. The mine, gift shop, and stamp mill open 10:00 A.M.– 4:00 P.M., mid-April–October.

Mine only open weekends noon–4:00 P.M., November–mid-April.

Info: The Gold Bug Mine is a typical area hardrock mine open for general admission and guided tours. Pan for gold in a trough.

For information on the Gold Bug Mine Tour, see the listing under Section 2.

Other services available: Mine tours, gift shop, picnic area, hiking trails.

Directions: Located one mile north of Highway 50 on Bedford Avenue in Placerville.

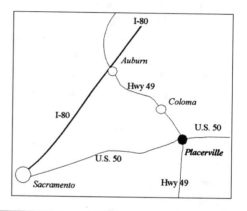

SECTION 2: Museums and Mine Tours

ALLEGHANY

Mine Tour/Museum 🏛

Underground Gold Miners Tours and Museum
P.O. Box 907
Alleghany, CA 95910
Phone: (530) 287-3330
E-mail: info@undergroundgold.com
www.origsix.com/ugmm.asp

Open: May through October by request. Call to make an appointment. Mine tours are by reservation only.

Info: Become a miner for a day as you explore huge quartz veins with one of today's miners. Half-day tour covers the surface operations of the Sixteen to One Mine and goes part way into the mine. The tour also includes the museum and the stamp mill. Full-day tours include lunch and travel into the main portal to the 800-foot level, historic areas of the mine, and the museum. The miner's working tour includes a trip in the man-skip to the depths of the mining operation. The executive tour is guided by the president of the corporation or the mining superintendent and includes the most active areas of the mine. Participate in the day's gold discoveries and learn about cutting-edge technology in mining.

A student's educational journey is also available, allowing students to experience California mining history and see first-hand underground geological formations.

The Underground Gold Miners Museum is committed to preserving and celebrating the gold miners' culture through the gathering of mining artifacts, historic photography, and the oral and written history of the period.

Admission: Museum is free. Underground tour (~ 4 hours) $95.00 (minimum of 2 required), miner's working tour $300.00, executive tour $600.00. Group discounts available. Children ½ price when accompanied by an adult.

Educational journey costs: Groups of 10–19, students and adults $55.00 each, groups of 20 or more students $30.00, adults $40.00 each.

Directions: All tours start from the Underground Gold Miners Museum, located on Main Street in Alleghany.

ANGELS CAMP

Museum

Angels Camp Museum & Carriage House
753 S. Main Street
Angels Camp, CA 95222
Phone: (209) 736-2963
Fax: (209) 736-0709
www.cityofangels.org/museum.htm

Open: All year; closed major holidays. 10:00 A.M.–3:00 P.M. daily, March–December; January–February, weekends only.

Info: The museum features a large display of rocks and minerals and a working model of a stamp mill and mining equipment. It houses 31 carriages and

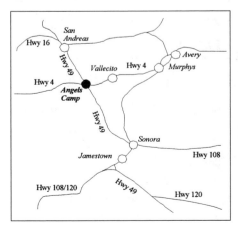

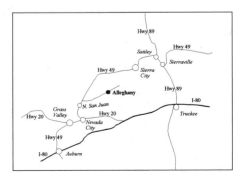

wagons. Picnic under native oaks on the banks of Chinese Gulch, where the 49ers panned for gold.

Admission: Adults $2.00, children (6–12) $0.50.

Directions: On Highway 49, ½ mile north of downtown Angels Camp.

AVALON

Museum

Catalina Island Museum Society, Inc.
One Casino Way
Casino Building
P.O. Box 366
Avalon, CA 90704
Phone: (310) 510-2414
www.ecatalina.com

Open: Every day of the year, 10:00 A.M.– 4:00 P.M.

Info: The museum has exhibits of artifacts relating to the mining conducted on Catalina Island since the 1860s, as well as representative rocks and minerals. Early mining on Catalina Island was focused on silver, rather than gold; the lack of water and easy land access affected the mining activities. Later mining produced silver, lead, and zinc, and quarries produced Catalina "marble" and shale.

Exhibits include: stone collection cut and polished for the Catalina Exhibit at the Chicago World's Fair in 1934; galena crystals; Catalina "marble"; and a variety of mining artifacts.

Admission: Call for fees.

Directions: In Avalon on Catalina Island.

BORON

Museum

Borax Visitor Center
Borax Global
14486 Borax Road
Boron, CA 93516
Phone: (760) 762–7588; (760) 762-7432

Open: All year (closed major holidays). 7 days a week, 9:00 A.M.–5:00 P.M.

Info: Discover the story of borax, a mineral formed over millions of years and valued since ancient times. From the center you can watch real mining operations in action. See the original 20-mule-team wagons that carried borax through the desert.

Admission: Cars $2.00, buses $10.00, motorcycles: $1.00.

Directions: Off State Highway 58 in Boron. Exit: Borax Road. Go north.

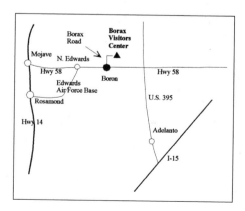

BORON

Museum

Boron Twenty Mule Team Museum
Boron Chamber of Commerce
26962 Twenty Mule Team Road
Boron, CA 93516
Phone: (760) 762-5810
Fax: (760) 762-0012
www.20muleteammuseum.org
www.boronchamber.org

Open: All year, 10:00 A.M.– 4:00 P.M.; closed major holidays.

Info: The museum features exhibits, both indoor and outdoor, that represent the history of the area and its mining. Learn the story of borax and the 20-mule-team wagons used to haul borate from Death Valley to the Mojave railroad, a distance of 165 miles across the desert.

Admission: Donation.

Directions: Boron is in southern California in the middle of the Mojave desert, 30 miles west of Barstow and 30 miles east of Mojave on State Highway 58.

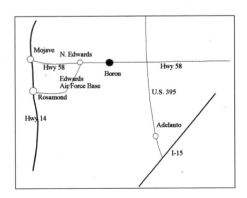

COLOMA

Museum

Marshall Gold Discovery State Historic Park
310 Back Street, P.O. Box 265
Coloma, CA 95613
Phone: (530) 622-3470 (park);
(530) 622-1116 (museum)

Open: Park open daily 8:00 A.M.–sunset. Museum open every day except Christmas and New Year's Day, 10:00 A.M.– 4:30 P.M.

Info: James Marshall discovered gold in January 1848 in the tailrace (the channel that carried water from the sawmill) from Sutter's Sawmill. This discovery started the great 1849 California Gold Rush.

Coloma's many historic sites, monuments, and buildings include the following:
• The Gold Discovery Museum, where the visitor center offers information, exhibits, and artifacts relating to the gold discovery and Gold Rush.

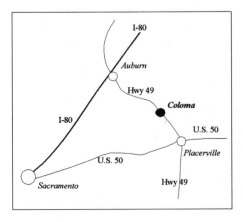

- The Mining Exhibit contains examples of some of the many kinds of equipment used by the miners. Three classic methods of gold mining are depicted: placer, hard-rock, and hydraulic mining.
- The Discovery Location, where gold was found by James Marshall in 1848. Today a quiet lagoon, a remnant of the original tailrace, marks the spot.
- Sutter's Sawmill, an accurate replica of the original mill.
- The Chinese Store, two restored buildings that house displays.

A brochure on historic tours is available from the park.

Admission: $5.00 per car.

Directions: The park is located along Main Street (Highway 49) in Coloma.

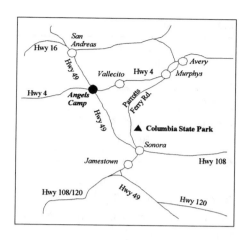

COLUMBIA

Mine Tour 🏛

Hidden Treasure Gold Mine
Matelot Gold Mine Supply Store
Columbia State Historic Park
Main Street, P.O. Box 28
Columbia State Park, CA 95310
Phone: (209) 532-9693 or
(209) 553-3105

Open: 7 days/week in summer weather permitting. Store opens at 10:00 A.M.; first tour at 11:00 A.M. unless prior arrangements have been made. Days/times vary in the winter; call ahead.

Info: The Hidden Treasure Gold Mine is an active working gold mine open to the public. Initially discovered in 1879, it still produces pockets of gold today. Visitors to the mine can see the gold-bearing quartz vein being mined.

The guided tour takes you through 800 feet of hardrock gold mine tunnels. During the tour, you'll discover what "stopes," "side drifts," and "glory holes" are all about.

Please note that the average temperature in the mine is 54°F, so dress appropriately. Tours leave from the Matelot Gold Mine Supply Store.

Rates: Adults $12.00, children 12 and under $10.00. Need minimum of six paid to go.

Directions: Located on Parrotts Ferry Road, just north of Sonora on State Highway 49 or just east of Angels Camp on State Highway 4. Follow signs. Tour office is located at the corner of Main and Washington Streets within Columbia State Historic Park.

DEATH VALLEY

Museum

Furnace Creek Borax Museum
P.O. Box 567
Death Valley, CA 92328
Phone: (760) 786-2345

Open: Daily, 8:00 A.M.– 4:30 P.M.;
45-minute closure at lunch.

Info: The Furnace Creek Borax Museum is a small museum but has some very interesting displays, both inside the building and on the surrounding grounds. The building itself was built in 1883 in Twenty Mule Team Canyon by Pacific Coast Borax Company and was moved to its present location in 1954 to house the museum. It is the oldest building in Death Valley.

The museum has a very fine rock and mineral collection that was the private collection of Harry Gower, chief geologist for Pacific Coast Borax Company and later head of the Land Department. He was with the company for 40 years, and the museum was formed under his leadership. Three of the showcases are devoted to just the borate minerals.

Buildings and grounds are handicapped accessible.

Admission: Free; outside tour guide is $1.50 plus tax.

Directions: The museum is located at Furnace Creek Ranch in Death Valley National Park in southern California, near the border with Nevada. Take State Highway 127 north from I-15 at Baker, then take State Highway 190 west at Death Valley Junction to Furnace Creek, or take Highway 190 east from U.S. 395 at Olancha to Death Valley.

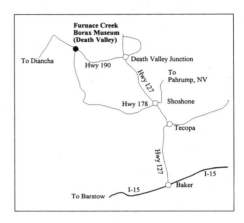

EL CAJON

Museum

Heritage of the Americas Museum
Cuyamaca College
12110 Cuyamaca College Drive West
El Cajon, CA 92019
Phone: (619) 670-5194

Open: Tuesday–Friday 10:00 A.M.– 4:00 P.M. Saturday 12:00–4:00 P.M. Closed selected holidays.

Info: The museum is located on the campus of Cuyamaca College in El Cajon. Its natural history wing has displays of rocks, minerals, meteorites, and quartz crystals.

Admission: Adults $3.00, children under 17 free with adult, seniors (65+) $2.00.

Directions: Use Cuyamaca College Drive West exit from Jamacha Road in Rancho San Diego.

FALLBROOK

Museum 🏛

Fallbrook Gem and Mineral Society Museum
123 W. Alvarado
Fallbrook, CA 92028
Phone: (760) 723-1130

Open: Thursday 1:00–5:00 P.M., and the second Sunday of every month 1:00 – 4:00 P.M.

Info: Features galleries of minerals from San Diego County, including beautifully colored tourmaline from local mines. Also has displays of minerals from around the world.

Note: Pink and green tourmaline from local mines were carved in the years of the Chinese Manchu dynasty. Also mined locally were rubies and other gems. In addition, mineral specimens are available for sale.

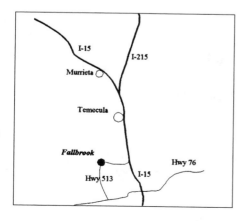

Admission: Free.

Directions: Fallbrook is just west of I-15 on State Highway S 13.

GRASS VALLEY

Museum 🏛

Empire Mine State Historic Park
10791 E. Empire Street
Grass Valley, CA 95945
Phone: (530) 273-8522

Open: September–April, 10:00 A.M.– 5:00 P.M. May–August, 9:00 A.M.–6:00 P.M.

Info: The Empire Mine State Historic Park is the site of the oldest and richest hardrock gold mine in California. In 1850, George Roberts discovered gold in a quartz outcropping, which became the Ophir vein. Word spread that hardrock gold had been found in California, and miners from tin and copper mines in Cornwall, England, flocked to the area. These men provided the bulk of the labor throughout the mine's history. The Empire Mine State Historic Park enables visitors to understand and appreciate the importance and fascinating story of hardrock mining.

Features:

- Look down the shaft of the oldest and richest gold mine in California.
- Browse through the historic mine yard.
- Stroll through the formal gardens of the wealthy mine owner.
- Hike the trails of the Empire back country with a self-guiding brochure to describe the sites along the way.
- Take a tour, and see a mining movie;

participate in the interpretive program; enjoy mine yard living history reenactment.

Admission: Adults $3.00, children 6–12 $1.00, children under 6 free.

Directions: Drive 24 miles north of Auburn on Highway 49 to Empire Street exit in Grass Valley. The park is located in Grass Valley at 10791 E. Empire Street.

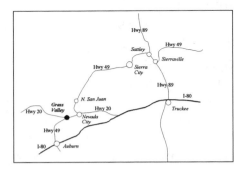

JACKSON

Museum 🏛

Amador County Museum
500 Argonaut Lane
Jackson, CA 95642-9534
Phone: (209) 223-6386

Open: Wednesday–Sunday, 10:00 A.M.– 4:00 P.M.

Info: The museum has a collection of mineral spheres, 16 of which are from California, including one made from gold ore quartz from Jackson. Spheres from California include calcite, chert, Chinese writing rock, cinnabar, granite, howlite, idacrase, jasper, matrix opal, myrakite, ulexite, quartz (gold ore), rice rock, rose quartz, rhodonite, and schor

sheen obsidian. The other spheres are from Utah and Nevada. Take a trip back to 1920 and see the Kennedy Mine in full operation through the magic of large-scale working models. The models, built by Robert Post, demonstrate the various functions of the headframe hoisting equipment, the stamp mill, and the famous Jackson Wheels. Hourly tours on Saturday and Sunday from 11:00 A.M.–3:00 P.M.

Admission: Free; donations appreciated. Model mine tour $1.00.

Directions: Jackson is located at the intersection of State Highway 49 and State Highway 88. The museum is located at 225 Church Street in Jackson.

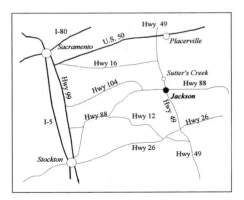

JACKSON

Mine Tour 🏛

Kennedy Gold Mine Tours
P.O. Box 684
Jackson, CA 95642-0684
Phone: (209) 223-9542

Open: Mid-March–October 31, weekends only. Tours from 10 A.M.–3 P.M.

Info: The Kennedy Mine was started in the 1850s, and was the deepest gold mine in North America when it was closed in 1942. A guided surface tour lasting 1 to 1½ hours is available. A self-guided tour explains the historic gold mine. Visitors can see the 125-foot head frame, tour several mine buildings, and try gold panning in the Kennedy Mine troughs.

Admission: Adults $9.00. Group tours with reservations.

Directions: Jackson is located at the intersection of State Highway 49 and State Highway 88.

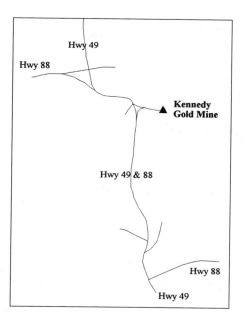

JULIAN

Mine Tour 🏛

Eagle & High Peak Gold Mine Tours
Eagle Mining Company
P.O. Box 624
Julian, CA 92036
Phone: (760) 765-0036

Open: 7 days/week, 10:00 A.M.–2:30 P.M. Hours may vary.

Info: The Eagle and High Peak Mines were started in 1870. A guided tour takes you through 1,000 feet of underground hardrock gold mine tunnel, past displays of period tools and machinery, and gold panning demonstrations. During the tour you will see the gold-bearing quartz vein, the gold extraction process, and antique trucks and equipment.

Admission: Adults $8.00, children $4.00, under 5 $1.00. Group tours with reservations.

Directions: Take C street in Julian north five blocks.

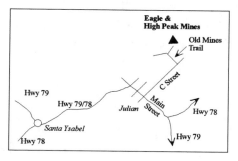

JULIAN

Museum

Julian Pioneer Museum
Julian Woman's Club
P.O. Box 511
2811 Washington Street
Julian, CA 92036
Phone: (760) 765-0227

Open: December–March, weekends and legal holidays; April–November, daily. Closed Thanksgiving, Christmas, New Year's Day, and during heavy snows. Hours: 10:00 A.M.– 4:00 P.M.

Info: Located in gold-mining country, the Julian Pioneer Museum has a good display of mining equipment and tools. Displays include assay equipment; the rock breaker invented and patented by Julian's founders, Drury D. Bailey and James O. Bailey; a "Long-Tom" rocker, and many others. The museum also has a rock and mineral display.

Admission: Adults $3.00, children under 7 free.

Directions: Julian is located northeast of San Diego, on State Highway 78.

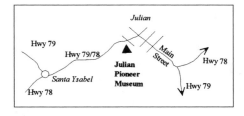

INDEPENDENCE

Museum

Eastern California Museum
155 North Grant Street
P.O. Box 206
Independence, CA 93526
Phone: (760) 878-0258
E-mail: ecmuseum@usamedia.tv
www.countyofinyo.org/ecmuseum/ecmdhome.htm

Open: 10:00 A.M.–4:00 P.M.; closed Tuesdays and major holidays. Times open may vary. Call ahead.

Info: The museum has a small but well-rounded regional gem and mineral collection.

Admission: Free; donations appreciated.

Directions: The museum is located 3 blocks west of U.S. 395, at 155 North Grant Street, in Independence.

LAKEPORT

Museum

Historic Courthouse Museum
255 N. Main Street
Lakeport, CA 95453
Phone: (707) 263-4555
www.museum.co.lake.ca.us

Open: Wednesday–Saturday, 11:00 A.M.– 4:00 P.M. Sunday, noon–4:00 P.M.

Info: The museum has an interesting display of minerals and gems found in Lake

County, including Lake County "diamonds," obsidian, jasper, quartz, chert, sulfur crystals, agate, rhyolite, serpentine, and cinnabar. A new gem and mineral museum will be open in early 2006.

Admission: Adults $2.00, children $1.00.

Directions: The Lake County Museum is located on Main Street between 2nd and 3rd Streets. Take either the Lakeport Boulevard or 11th Street exits from Hwy. 29 to Main Street. The museum is in the center of town.

LOS ANGELES

Museum

Natural History Museum of
Los Angeles County
Mineral Sciences Dept.
900 Exposition Boulevard
Los Angeles, CA 90007
Phone: (213) 763-3466 (general);
(213) 763-3328 (mineral science dept.)
Fax: (213) 749-4107
E-mail: akampf@nhm.org
www.nhm.org/research/minsci

Open: Monday–Friday, 9:30 A.M.–5:00 P.M. Saturday and Sunday 10:00 A.M.–5:00 P.M.

Info: The Mineral Sciences collection includes minerals, rocks, meteorites, gems and related synthetic materials. The collection includes more than 150,000 specimens, including approximately 140,000 minerals (including 12 types and 100,000 micromounts) 3,000 rocks, 3,000 gems, and 45 meteorites. It is said that in overall significance, the collection probably ranks 4th in the U.S. The collection is worldwide in scope, with a specialization in California.

The Hall of Gems and Minerals features:
- Minerals of California, with superb specimens from the southern California pegmatites, including topaz, tourmaline, kunzite, morganite, and quartz
- Nearly 400 native gold specimens
- Basics of mineralogy exhibit
- Systematic mineralogy exhibit: nearly 500 specimens from around the world demonstrate the systematic classification of minerals
- Specimens to touch, including rocks, minerals, and meteorites
- Gem carvings
- Hixon Gem Vault houses one of the finest collections of gemstones on public display west of Washington, D.C.; this display includes a suite of sapphires and rubies of virtually every color.

Admission: Adults $9.00, seniors and children (13–17) $6.50, children (5–12) $2.00. First Tuesday of each month is free.

Directions: The museum is located in Exposition Park in Los Angeles, which is adjacent to I-110 (Harbor Freeway).

MARIPOSA

Museum

California State Mining and Mineral
Museum
P.O. Box 1192
Mariposa, CA 95338
Phone: (209) 742-7625
E-mail: rockmuseum@sti.net

Open: All year. Summer (May 1–
September 30), 10:00 A.M.–6:00 P.M.
Winter (October 1– April 30),
10:00 A.M.– 4:00 P.M., closed Tuesdays.
Info: Features gold, California's mining
heritage. See gold in its native forms,
including gold nuggets and crystallized
gold, as well as gems and minerals from
around the world.
Admission: Adults $3.00, children
under 16 free. Call for free tours or
school programs.
Directions: 1.8 miles south of Mariposa
on State Route 49 at the County Fair-
grounds. One hour away from Yosemite
on Hwy. 140.

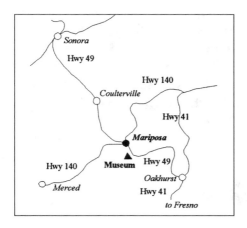

NEEDLES

Museum

Needles Regional Museum
929 Front Street
P.O. Box 978
Needles, CA 92363
Phone: (760) 326-5678
www.needlesmuseum@frontiernet.net

Open: All year, 10:00 A.M.–2:00 P.M.,
closed July–August.
Info: Small collection of specimens
includes "Needles blue agate" and Colorado river pebble terrace stones.
Admission: Free, donations accepted.
Directions: 929 Front Street, across the
Santa Fe Park from the historic train
station.

NEVADA CITY

Museum

Malakoff Diggins Park Association
Malakoff Diggins State Historical Park
23579 N. Bloomfield Road
Nevada City, CA 95959

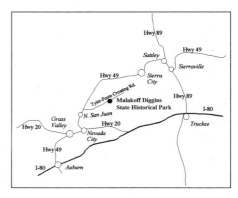

Phone: (530) 265-2740

Open: Park open all year, daily. Call prior to arrival; conditions may vary. Museum open Memorial Day–Labor Day, daily 10:00 A.M.–4:30 P.M.; open weekends only in spring and fall.

Info: Malakoff Diggins State Historical Park tells the story of the "free-for-all" hydraulic gold mining era in California. Hydraulic mining consisted of blasting a hillside with a stream of water until the soil disintegrated. The muddy stream was then directed down a sluice that caught the heavier gold-bearing particles of soil and gravel. The remaining mud went into a stream or river, or wherever it could flow.

Displays and a movie in the park museum tell the story of hydraulic mining and the miner's lives. Walking trails lead to the great Malakoff mine pit, 7,000 feet by 3,000 feet, and as deep as 600 feet in places. During the summer, rangers conduct tours of the North Bloomfield townsite daily and gold panning tours on weekends.

Admission: $6.00/developed parking.

Other services available: Family camping, group camping, cabins, fishing, hiking, swimming.

Directions: From Nevada City, travel 11 miles north on Highway 49 toward Downieville. Turn right onto Tyler Foote Road, stay on the pavement and follow the yellow line to the park. The road changes names a few times (Curzon Grade Road, Back Bone Road, Derbec Road, N. Bloomfield Road). These are not high speed roads. The park is 26 miles from Nevada City.

PACIFIC GROVE

Museum 🏛

Pacific Grove Museum of Natural History
165 Forest Avenue
Pacific Grove, CA 93950
Phone: (831) 648-5716
Fax: (831) 372-3256
E-mail: pgmuseum@mbay.net
www.pgmuseum.org

Open: All year, 10:00 A.M.–5:00 P.M. Tuesday–Saturday. Group tours must have reservations.

Info: The museum has a large exhibit on general geology and mineralogy. Included is a display of Monterey County rocks and structural geology. An enclosed booth is devoted to fluorescent minerals. There is also a new exhibit on California jade.

Admission: Free.

Other services available: Gift shop.

Directions: Located in downtown Pacific Grove at the intersection of Forest and Central Avenues.

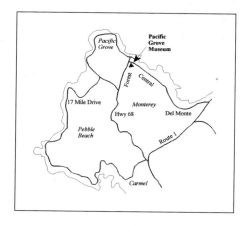

PASO ROBLES

Museum

El Paso de Robles Area Pioneer
Museum
2010 Riverside Avenue, P.O. Box 461
Paso Robles, CA 93447
Phone: (805) 239-4556
www.pasoroblespioneer.museum.org

Open: Thursday–Sunday, 1:00 – 4:00 P.M.
Info: The rock and mineral display at the
museum includes local minerals as well as
photographs and maps of old mines in
the area. It was established and is main-
tained by the Santa Lucia Rockhounds
(P.O. Box 1672, Paso Robles, CA 93447).
Admission: Free; donations appreciated.
Directions: South of mid-state fair-
grounds on Riverside Avenue in Paso
Robles.

PLACERVILLE

Mine Tour/Museum

Hangtown's Gold Bug Park & Mine
2635 Gold Bug Lane
Placerville, CA 95667
Phone: (530) 642-5207
Guided Group Tours Line: (503) 642-
5238
www.goldbugpark.org

Open: Daily from mid-April–October,
10:00 A.M.– 4:00 P.M. Mine only open
November–March, 12:00– 4:00 P.M. Picnic and hiking areas open all year
8:30 A.M.– 5:00 P.M., weather permitting.

Info: The Gold Bug Mine is a horizon-
tal drift hardrock mine of the mother
lode now open to the public for self-
guided tours. Temperature in the mine is
about 55°F, so you should dress accordingly. Hard hats are provided.

Also available at the park is the Joshua
Hendy Stamp Mill, built as a communi-
ty ore crusher, and gem and mineral dis-
plays. The Hattie Museum and Gift
Shop has exhibits and displays that
explain the neighborhood mining area.
Admission: Adults $4.00, children 7–16
$2.00, under 6 free.
Other services available: Gift shop,
picnic area, hiking trails.
Directions: One mile north from State
Highway 50 on Bedford Avenue.

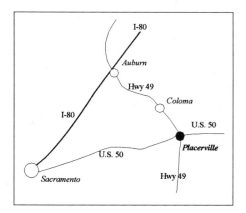

QUINCY

Museum

Plumas County Museum
500 Jackson Street
Quincy, CA 95971
Phone: (530) 283-6320

Open: Tuesday–Saturday 8:00 A.M.–5:00 P.M., Sunday 10:00 A.M.–4:00 P.M., May 1–September 30.

Info: Gold and copper mining were the predominant industries in the history of the county, and the museum has a large number of documents and artifacts relating to the mining of these minerals.

Admission: Adults $2.00, children 12–17 $0.50, children under 12 free.

Directions: 500 Jackson Street in Quincy.

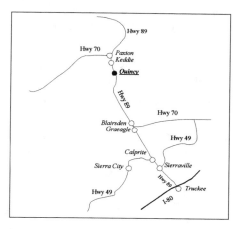

history of the Palos Verdes Peninsula.

Admission: Adult $2.00, children/seniors/handicapped $1.00.

Other services available: Picnic area, walking path, whale watching, guided tours, including geology and tidal pool tours.

Directions: Take Palos Verdes Drive West from Highway 101 (Pacific Coast Highway). The center is located next to the Pointe Vicente Light House.

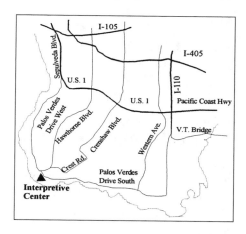

RANCHO PALOS VERDES

Museum 🏛

Pointe Vicente Interpretive Center
31501 Palos Verdes Drive West
Rancho Palos Verdes, CA 90275
Phone: (310) 377-5370

Open: All year, winter 10:00 A.M.–5:00 P.M. daily, summer 10:00 A.M.–7:00 P.M. daily. Closed major holidays.

Info: The Interpretive Center's museum has exhibits on the geology and natural

REDLANDS

Museum 🏛

San Bernardino County Museum
2024 Orange Tree Lane
Redlands, CA 92374-4560
Phone: (909) 307-2669
www.co.san-bernadino.ca.us/museum/

Open: Tuesday–Sunday, 9:00 A.M.–5:00 P.M. Closed major holidays.

Info: The museum's collection of rocks, minerals, and gems contains more than

45,000 catalogued specimens.

Admission: Adults $6.00, students and seniors $5.00, children 5–12 $4.00, children under 5 free.

Other services available: Picnic area, gift shop.

Directions: Take the California Street exit from I-10 in Redlands.

RIDGECREST

Museum

Maturango Museum
100 East Las Flores Avenue
Ridgecrest, CA 93555
Phone: (760) 375-6900
www.maturango.org

Open: Daily 10:00 A.M.–5:00 P.M. Closed for major holidays.

Info: The museum has a small but well-rounded regional gem and mineral collection, containing both natural and polished specimens of the surrounding region.

Admission: Adults $4.00, children, military, and senior citizens $2.00, children under 6 free.

Directions: At the corner of Las Flores Avenue and Ridgecrest Boulevard.

RIVERSIDE

Museum

Jurupa Mountains Cultural Center
7621 Granite Hills Drive
Riverside, CA 92509

Phone: (909) 685-5818
E-mail: info@the-jmcc.org
www.the-jmcc.org

Open: Tuesday–Saturday 8:00 A.M.–4:30 P.M.

Info: Public tours on Saturdays only. Dinosaur Walks at 9:00 A.M. and 1:30 P.M. are guided tours which take 1½ hours and include a program, nature walk, and collecting twelve different rocks and fossils. Earth Science Museum with displays of rocks, minerals, fluorescent minerals, and more. Now on display is the largest dinosaur egg collection (from China) in the U.S.

Admission: $6.00 per person (adults and children); children under 2 are free. No charge for admission to museum.

Directions: From Mission Boulevard, turn north on Camino Real, to the center.

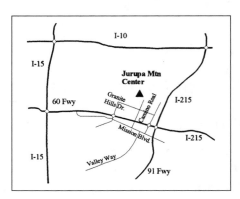

RIVERSIDE

Museum

Riverside Metropolitan Museum
3580 Mission Inn Avenue

Riverside, CA 92501
Phone: (951) 826-5273
www.riversideca.gov/museum

Open: All year, 9:00 A.M.–5:00 P.M. Tuesday–Friday, 10:00 A.M.–5:00 P.M. Saturday, 11:00 A.M.–5:00 P.M. Sunday. Closed Mondays and major holidays.

Info: The museum features natural history exhibits featuring rocks, minerals, gems, and geology of the region.

Admission: Free.

Other services available: Gift shop.

Directions: Call for directions. The Metropolitan Museum is located on Mission Inn Avenue, one block east from where Main Street crosses Mission Inn Avenue.

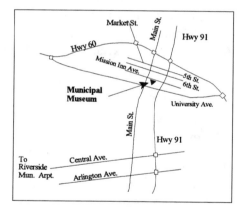

RIVERSIDE

Museum

World Museum of Natural History
La Sierra University
4700 Pierce Street
Riverside, CA 92505

Phone: (951) 785-2209

Open: All year, Wednesday mornings during the academic year, 2:00–5:00 P.M. Saturday. Other days by appointment.

Features:

• Fluorescent minerals display. (Did you know that when activated by ultraviolet radiation, certain minerals with trace inclusions will transmit visible light? The color TV picture tube is a commercial application.)

• Meteorite display, including recent California finds.

• Tektite display. The tektites that are found across Australia and Southeast Asia are believed to come from the impact on the moon that created the Tycho Crater.

• Collection of over 1,300 mineral spheres, including the large verde antique sphere from Victorville, which weighs 396 pounds.

• Minerals from around the world.

Admission: Free; donations are accepted.

Directions: Call for directions.

SAN DIEGO

Museum 🏛

San Diego Natural History Museum
1788 El Prado
Balboa Park
San Diego, CA 92101
Phone: (619) 232-3821
www.sdnhm.org

Open: Daily, 10:00 A.M.– 5:00 P.M.

Info: Museum collection has 26,000 mineral specimens, but only a few are on public display. The mineralogy collection is mostly the result of work by dedicated community collectors, notably Josephine Scripps, and houses an excellent collection of the valuable minerals found in San Diego County mines in pegmatite deposits.

Admission: Adults $9.00, children (3–17) $5.00, seniors, military $6.00.

Directions: The museum is located at the east end of Balboa Park.

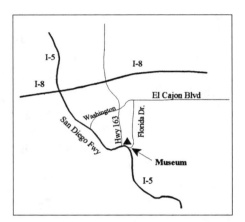

SANTA BARBARA

Museum

Department of Earth Sciences
University of California–Santa Barbara
Santa Barbara, CA 93106
Phone: (805) 893-3477

Open: All year, 7:00 A.M.–5:00 P.M. during academic year, Monday–Thursday.

Info: Several collections and exhibits are on display in the department. The showpiece is an international award-winning gem and mineral collection donated in 1997 by Edward Bancroft. The collection consists of 67 samples displayed in a custom case designed to highlight the minerals' natural colors. In addition to the Bancroft collection, there is a real-time display of southern California seismic activity, as well as displays on the local geology and geological history, samples of mid–ocean ridge hydrothermal vents (black smokers) and tube worms, and an older mineral collection showing minerals and their tectonic settings. The department also owns large research collections of minerals and rocks. These collections are not on display but can be viewed by groups with proper arrangements.

Admission: Free.

Directions: Call or write for directions.

SHOSHONE

Museum

Shoshone Museum
P.O. Box 38, Highway 127
Shoshone, CA 92384
Phone: (760) 852-4414

Open: All year, summer: 7:00 A.M.–4:00 P.M., winter 8:00 A.M.–4:00 P.M., 7 days/week.

Info: The museum's rock collection is extensive and reflects the geology of the region.

Admission: Call for fees.

Directions: On the edge of Death Valley, at the southeast entrance to the National Park.

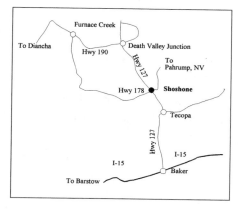

Directions: Half a mile east of Sierra City on State Highway 49, in Sierra County Historical Park.

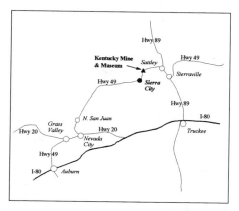

SIERRA CITY

Museum 🏛

Kentucky Mine and Museum
Sierra County Historical Society
P.O. Box 260
Sierra City, CA 96125
Phone: (530) 862-1310
Fax: (530) 862-1310
E-mail: kentuckymine@telis.org

Open: Memorial Day–late September, 10:00 A.M.–5:00 P.M., Wednesday–Sunday.
Info: The museum has both inside and outside exhibits on the gold and mercury mining in the area. Exhibits include a rocker used in placer mining, riffles used in ground sluicing, a hoist cage, and a 10-stamp mill.
Admission: $1.00.
Tours: Adults $5.00, children 7–17 $2.50, 6 and under free.

SONORA

Museum 🏛

Tuolumne County Museum
158 W. Bradford Avenue, P.O. Box 299
Sonora, CA 95370-0299
Phone: (209) 532-1317
www.tchistory.org/museum.html

Open: All year, 10:00 A.M.– 4:00 P.M.
Info: The museum is located in what was formerly a jail which dates back to 1857. Displays of county history, including mining during the Gold Rush, fill the front gallery while Justice and the Law, mid-19th-century emigrant crossings of the Sierra Nevada, antique firearms, and an old time gun shop are in the two cell blocks.
Admission: Donation.
Directions: In Sonora on West Bradford two blocks off Highway 49.

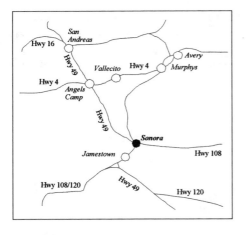

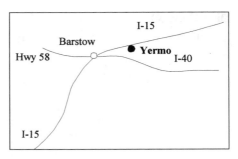

Directions: Located just off I-15, midway between Los Angeles and Las Vegas, 10 miles north of Barstow. Calico is 8 miles north of Barstow on Ghost Town Road.

YERMO

Mine Tour

Calico Ghost Town
P.O. Box 638
Yermo, CA 92398
Phone: (760) 254-2122;
(800) TO-CALICO (862-2542)
Fax: (760) 254-2047

Open: All year except Christmas, 7 days/ week. Town: 8:00 A.M.–dusk. Shops: 9:00 A.M.–5:00 P.M.

Info: Calico Ghost Town is a San Bernardino County Park, with an old silver mine that can be explored, and an 1880s silver "boom town" with a wide variety of shops.

Admission: Adults $6.00, children 6–15 $3.00, children under 6 free. Tour groups are offered special rates by calling ahead.

Other services available: Restaurants, rail tour, 110-unit campground, cabins or bunkhouse accommodations, horseback riding.

YREKA

Museum 🏛

Siskiyou County Courthouse
311 4th Street
Yreka, CA 96097-2912
Phone: (530) 842-3836

Open: Weekdays 9:00 A.M.–5:00 P.M.

Info: Located at the Siskiyou County courthouse is an impressive display of gold nuggets, gold-containing quartz rock, gold dust, jewelry, and other artifacts, all of which can be traced to Siskiyou County sources, with an estimated value of over $1,000,000. The display is maintained by the Siskiyou County Museum, which also has a small display of its own.

Admission: Free.

Directions: Yreka is on I-5, 20 miles south of the California–Oregon border.

YUCCA VALLEY

Museum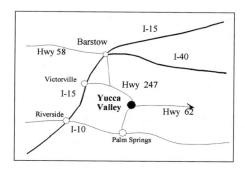

Hi-Desert Nature Museum
57090 Twentynine Palms Highway
Yucca Valley, CA 92284
Phone: (760) 369-7212
www.yucca-valley.org/services/
museum.html

Open: All year, 10:00 A.M.–5:00 P.M., Tuesday–Sunday. Closed major and national holidays.

Info: The museum's rock and mineral collection includes a special viewing room for fluorescent minerals.

Admission: Free, donations appreciated.
Other services available: Museum shop.
Directions: The museum is part of the Town of Yucca Valley Community Center Complex located on Dumosa Avenue in the north side of State Highway 62 in Yucca Valley.

SECTION 3: Special Events and Tourist Information

ANNUAL EVENT

Rock Bonanza, Boron, CA

Occurs the weekend before Easter. Guides take you out to collecting areas. U.S. Borax allows collecting in their "dumps," and good borate samples can be found.

For more information:
Boron Chamber of Commerce
26962 Twenty Mule Team Road
Boron, CA 93516-1560
Phone: (760) 762-5810

Hosting Club:
Mojave Mineralogical Society
P.O. Box 511

Boron, CA 93596
Phone: (760) 762-6422

ANNUAL EVENT

Gold Rush Days, Coloma, CA

Held during the second week of October each year.

Volunteers and staff of Marshall Gold Discovery State Historic Park recreate the Gold Rush. Interactive trade demonstrations and living history activities feature music, 49er cooking, carpentry, doll-making, quilting, 1850s-era costumes, panning, spinning, weaving, pioneer crafts, and more. Other highlights include a wagon train and a prospector camp. A nugget race and other competitions take place, and special excursions to local Gold Rush towns, mines, and other places of interest are held. A Saturday night banquet includes entertainment and keepsake gifts.

For more information:
Marshall Gold Discovery State Historic Park
310 Back Street, P.O. Box 205
Coloma, CA 95613
Phone: (530) 622-3470

TOURIST INFORMATION

State Tourist Agency

California Tourism
P.O. Box 1499
Sacramento, CA 95812-1499
Phone: (916) 444-4429;
(800) TO CALIF (862-2543)
E-mail: info@cttc1.com
www.visitcalifornia.com

COLORADO

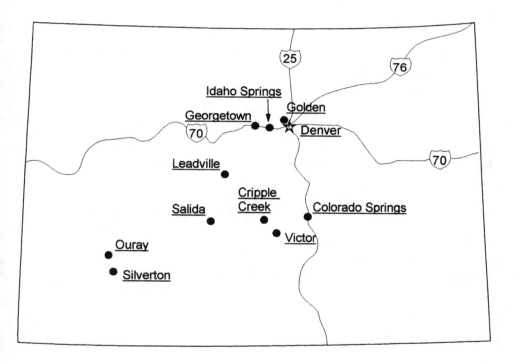

State Gemstone: Aquamarine
State Mineral: Rhodochrosite

IDAHO SPRINGS / *Enriched • Easy*

Pan for Gold or Gemstones 𝒯

The following gems or minerals may be found:

▪ **Gold, assorted gemstones**

Argo Gold Mill
P.O. Box 1990
Idaho Springs, CO 80452
Phone: (303) 567-2421
www.historicargotours.com

Open: April 15–October 15, 9:00 A.M.–6:00 P.M. 7 days a week.

Info: Tours of the mill and the Double Eagle Mine are also given at the Argo Gold Mill site. See entry in Section 2 for more information.

Rates: Guaranteed Placer Gold $6.00 or $10.00; guaranteed gemstones $6.00.

Directions: Located 32 miles west of Denver on I-70.

IDAHO SPRINGS / *Native •*
Moderate

Pan for Gold Along a Mountain Stream 𝒯

The following gems or minerals may be found:

▪ **Gold**

Phoenix Mine
P.O. Box 3236
Idaho Springs, CO 80452
Phone: (303) 567-0422
or call Idaho Springs Information
Center at (303) 567-4382
www.phoenixgoldmine.com

Open: All year, weather permitting, 10:00 A.M.–6:00 P.M.; closed at 5:00 P.M. during winter. Spring and summer, 7 days/week; winter, weekends only.

Info: Try out the old-time miner's tools and pan for gold in a beautiful mountain stream. Keep all that you find. For information on the underground mine tour, see Section 2.

Panning fee: $5.00; free for severely handicapped. Group tour by appointment.

Directions: I-70 exit 239 to Stanley Road west to Trail Creek Road, then south to Phoenix Mine.

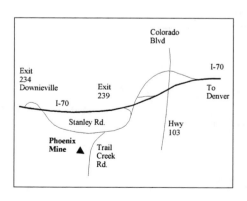

COLORADO SPRINGS

Museum

Western Museum of Mining & Industry
225 N. Gate Boulevard
Colorado Springs, CO 80921
Phone (719) 488-0880; (800) 752-6558
E-mail: info@wmmi.org
www.wmmi.org

Open: 9:00 A.M.–4:00 P.M., Monday–Saturday. Tours leave at 10:00 A.M. and 1:00 P.M.

Info: Brings the history of mining to life with daily guided tours, gold panning demonstrations, mining equipment displays, and a re-created mine. Mining equipment ranges from steam shovels to stamp mills to mine burros.

Admission: Adults $8.00, seniors 60+ and students 13+ $5.00, children 3–12 $3.00, children under 3 free.

Directions: Take I-25 to Exit 156A. Opposite the north entrance to the museum is the U.S. Air Force Academy.

CRIPPLE CREEK

Museum

Cripple Creek District Museum
5th & Bennet Avenue
P.O. Box 1210
Cripple Creek, CO 80813
Phone: (719) 689-9540; (719) 689-2634
E-mail: ccdistrictmuseum@aol.com
www.cripple-creek.org

Open: Daily, 10:00 A.M.–5:00 P.M., June 1–September 30; 10:00 A.M.–4:00 P.M., Friday–Sunday, October 1–May 30.

Info: The mission of the museum is to preserve the history of the fabulous Cripple Creek mining district. The Museum, located in a former railroad terminal, has six floors of mining memorabilia, maps, mineral displays, and other items reflecting the area's heritage.

Admission: Adults $5.00, military and seniors $3.00, children under 12 $2.50, children under 6 free. Group discounts available with prior reservations.

Directions: At the intersection of 5th Avenue and Bennett Avenue in Cripple Creek.

CRIPPLE CREEK

Mine Tour

Mollie Kathleen Gold Mine
State Route 67
Cripple Creek, CO
Phone: (719) 689-2466; (888) 291-5689, PIN 9101
www.goldminetours.com

Open: Daily, April–October, 9:00 A.M.–5:00 P.M.; November–March, 10:00 A.M.–4:00 P.M., Saturday–Sunday.

Info: Tour an historic underground gold mine. Two-compartment skips (small mine elevators) carry visitors 1,000 feet below the ground to the old mine workings, where there are displays of equipment that demonstrate the history of gold-mining in the Mollie Kathleen. Visitors receive a small piece of gold ore before leaving the mine.

Admission: Adults $15.00, children 5–14 $7.00.

Directions: The Mollie Kathleen Mine is located one mile north of Cripple Creek on State Route 67.

DENVER

Museum

Denver Museum of Nature and Science
2001 Colorado Boulevard
Denver, CO 80205
Phone: (303) 322-7009; (800) 925-2250
www.dmns.org

Open: All year, every day except Christmas, 9:00 A.M.–5:00 P.M.

Info: Over 2,000 fine specimens are on display in the Coors Gem and Mineral Hall. Included are crystallized gold and gold nuggets, topaz, aquamarine, and amazonite. Exhibits also show the history of Colorado minerals and mines. Significant contributions were made by amateur collectors.

Admission: Adults $10.00, children (3–8) and seniors 65+ $6.00.

Directions: The museum is located at the intersection of Colorado Boulevard and Montview Boulevard in City Park.

GEORGETOWN

Mine Tour

Lebanon Silver Mine
c/o Georgetown Loop Railroad, Inc.
P.O. Box 217
1111 Rose Street
Georgetown, CO 80444
Phone: (303) 569-1000; (888) RAILS4U
www.georgetownloop.com

Open: May–September, 7 days/week. Call for exact dates and times.

Info: Ride a narrow-gauge train to the Lebanon Silver Mine and then take a walking tour of the mine. Guides will take you through the mine, change

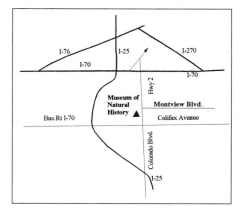

rooms, mine manager's office, blacksmith shop, and tool shed. The temperature in the mine is a constant 44°F, so wear a jacket or sweater. The mine tour can be reached only by train from the Silver Plume departure point; reservations are accepted from the Silver Plume departure point only. The tour is not available on the "Taste of Tahoe" car or on the last departure of the day from the Silver Plume departure point (I-70 exit 226).

Admission: Adults $6.00, children (3–15) $4.00.

Train Fares: Adults $16.50, children (3–15) $11.25.

Directions: Located 50 minutes west of Denver on I-70.

GOLDEN

Museum   🏛

Geology Museum
Colorado School of Mines
Golden, CO 80401-1887
Phone: (303) 273-3815
Fax: (303) 273-3859
Telex: 9109340190CSMGLDN
www.mines.edu/academic/geology/museum

Open: All year, 9:00 A.M.–4:00 P.M., Monday–Saturday, 1:00 – 4:00 P.M. Sunday. Closed Sundays in summer and Colorado School of Mines holidays. Tours may be scheduled.

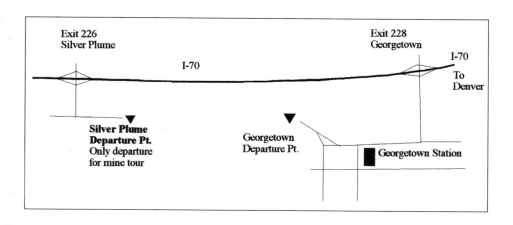

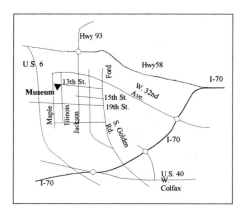

Info: The museum has a collection of approximately 50,000 mineral, gemstone, fossil, and artifact specimens.

Exhibits include: Minerals from around the world; Gemstones and precious metals; Colorado mining history; Blasters Uranium Mine; Earth history; Radiation center; Kids' corner.

Admission: Free; tours may be scheduled.

Directions: Located on the corner of 13th and Maple Streets in Golden.

IDAHO SPRINGS

Mine Tour/Museum 🏛 (National Historic Site)

Argo Gold Mill
P.O. Box 1990
Idaho Springs, CO 80452
Phone: (303) 567-2421
www.historicargotours.com

Open: April 15–October 15, 9:00 A.M.–6:00 P.M., 7 days/week. Last tour leaves at 4:30 P.M.

Info:

▪ Self-guided tour through the Argo Gold Mill, which was built to process 120 tons per day.

▪ Mine tour of the Double Eagle Mine. A mining museum that displays the tools and equipment used by the early miners of the 1800s and the more modern equipment used at the turn of the century. The museum also displays interesting mineral specimens found during mining.

▪ Gold and gemstone panning (see listing in Section 1).

Admission: Adults $14.00, children (7–12) $9.00.

Note: All paid admissions receive a small bag of gold ore to pan out with gold panning lesson.

Directions: Located 32 miles west of Denver on I-70.

IDAHO SPRINGS

Mine Tour

Edgar Experimental Mine
365 8th Avenue, P.O. Box 1184
Idaho Springs, CO 80452
Phone: (303) 567-2911
Fax: (303) 567-9133
E-mail: dmosh@miners.edu
www.mines.edu/academic/mining/
edgar.html

Open: Early June–late August. Call for tour time.

Info: The mine is a Colorado School of Mines experimental mine. In the 1870s it produced high-grade silver, gold, lead, and copper. Today it is used as an underground laboratory for future engineers who are being trained to find, develop, and process the world's material resources.

Admission: Adults $6.00, children 6–16 $3.00, children under 6 free, seniors $4.00.

Directions: The Edgar Mine is located in Idaho Springs, approximately 40 miles west of Denver. It can be reached by Interstate 70 or U.S. 6, taking Exit 240 north to Colorado Boulevard, turning west to 8th Avenue, where a sign marks the entrance road.

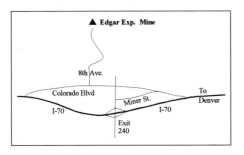

IDAHO SPRINGS

Mine Tour

Phoenix Mine
P.O. Box 3236
Idaho Springs, CO 80452
Phone: (303) 567-0422, or call
Idaho Springs Information Center at
(303) 567-4382
www.phoenixgoldmine.com

Open: All year, weather permitting, 10:00 A.M.–6:00 P.M.; closed at 5:00 P.M. during winter. Spring and summer, 7 days/week; winter, weekends only. Group tours by appointment.

Info: See a working underground hardrock mine where real miners still push tons of gold and silver ore in small rail cars just as they did 100 years ago. Take a personalized tour with a seasoned Colorado hardrock miner. Try old-timers' mining tools. Pan for gold (see listing in Section 1). Special school tours, which include a search for buried treasure, are given.

Admission: Adults $9.00, children under 12 $5.00, free for severely handicapped. Fee includes gold panning.

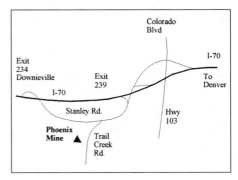

Directions: I-70 Exit 239 to Stanley Road west to Trail Creek Road, then south to Phoenix Mine.

LEADVILLE

Mine Tour

Matchless Mine
The Leadville Assembly, Inc.
414 W. 7th Street
Leadville, CO 80461
Phone: (719) 486-4918
www.matchlessmine.com

Open: 9:00 A.M.– 4:45 P.M.

Info: The Matchless Mine symbolizes the nearly unbelievable fortunes that could be made during the mining booms, and the seclusion and poverty that waited when the booms ended. The Matchless was purchased in 1879 for $117,000 and, over a 14-year period, generated as much as $1 million a year for its owner, H. A. W. Tabor. Yet, when the silver market crashed in the Silver Panic of 1893, Tabor and his wife, Baby Doe, were reduced to poverty, and died penniless. The cabin at the mine where Baby Doe kept a 36-year vigil waiting for the price of silver to recover has been restored and is open to the public, along with displays of personal artifacts.

Admission: Adults $3.50, children 6–12 $1.00, children under 6 free.

Directions: Leadville is located at State Highway 91 and U.S. 24. The Matchless Mine is located on 7th Street, 1¼ miles east of town.

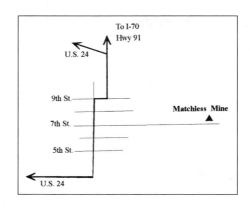

LEADVILLE

Museum

National Mining Hall of Fame and Museum
P.O. Box 981
120 W. 9th Street
Leadville, CO 80461
Phone: (719) 486-1229
Fax: (719) 486-3927
www.leadville.com/miningmuseum

Open: All year. May–October, daily 9:00 A.M.–5:00 P.M.; November–April, Monday–Saturday, 10:00 A.M.–4:00 P.M.

Info: Tells the story of the American mining industry from coal to gold. Displays include prospector's cave, a walk-through exhibit consisting of a wall of quartz crystals and pyrite specimens; K. C. Li magic room of industrial minerals, which educates visitors on the importance of mining in daily life; and diamonds from the Kelsey Lake dia-

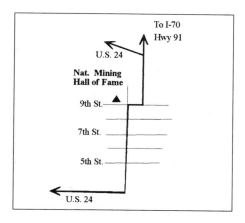

mond mine, near Fort Collins, CO, one of only two commercial diamond mines in North America.

Admission: Adults $6.00, seniors $5.00, children 6–12 $3.00, children under 6 free.

Directions: Leadville is located at State Highway 91 and U.S. 24. The museum is located on 9th Street, one block west.

OURAY

Museum

Ouray County Historical Society Museum
420 Sixth Avenue
Ouray, CO 81427
Phone: (970) 325-4576
www.ouraycountyhistoricalsociety.org

Open: Call for hours.

Info: Housed in the original St. Joseph's Miner's Hospital, there are 27 rooms on three floors. Displays feature mining, and include a large display of minerals.

Also at the complex is the W. Ross Moore Mining History Library of the American West.

Admission: Adults $5.00, seniors 60+ $3.50, children under 13 $1.00. Group rates are available.

Directions: 420 Sixth Avenue in Ouray.

SALIDA

Mine Tour 🏛

Lost Mine Tour
P.O. Box 3
Salida, CO 81201
Phone: (719) 221-MINE (6463)
(719) 539-7786
www.salida.com/lostmine

Open: Daily, May 15–September 30; October 1–May 14, Friday–Sunday. (Call 719-539-7786 to confirm that the mine is open.) Tours leave at 10:00 A.M. and 2:00 P.M.

Info: A 3-hour tour of a closed manganese mine in the rugged backcountry near Salida, CO. A four-wheel drive "Minemobile" takes you through a variety of geological and mining-related displays, then lets you off at the base of the hill leading to the mine portal. The walking portion of the tour takes you up and into the mine. The temperature in the mine is 50°F, so bring clothing with you.

Tour fee: Adults $45.00, children 5–12 $29.00.

Directions: The tours leave from either the Rock Shop (which is located between Salida and Buena Vista) or Earth Treasures of the Salida Museum, both in Salida. Advance reservations are recommended, particularly in the off-season.

SILVERTON

Gold Mill Tour 🏛

Mayflower Gold Mill
San Juan County Historical Society
P.O. Box 154
Silverton, CO 81433
Phone: (970) 387-5609
E-mail: silvertonarchive@aol.com
www.silvertonhistoricalsociety.org

Open: Memorial Day–mid-October, 10:00 A.M.–5:00 P.M. 7 days/week. Hours change mid-September.
Info: Tour the historic Mayflower Gold Mill. Tours leave every half hour.
Admission: Adults (13+) $8.00, seniors

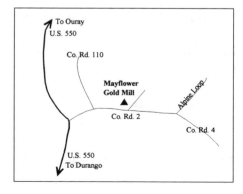

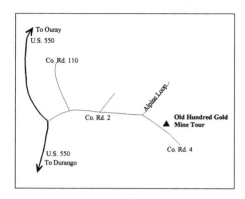

$5.50, children under 12 free.
Directions: Located east of Silverton on Highway East 110.

SILVERTON

Mine Tour 🏛

Old Hundred Gold Mine Tour, Inc.
P.O. Box 430
Silverton, CO 81433
Phone: (970) 387-5444; (800) 872-3009

Open: Mid-May–mid-October, 10:00 A.M.–4:00 P.M.; 7 days/week
Info: Ride a mine tram ⅓ mile underground and see live mining equipment demonstrations.. Tours leave hourly.
Admission: Adults $16.95, children (5–12) $7.95, children under 5 free if on lap, seniors over 60 $15.95.
Other services available: Picnic area, gift shop, snacks.
Directions: Located 5 miles east of Silverton on County Road 2; turn right on County Road 4 (follow signs).

SILVERTON

Museum

San Juan County Historical Society
Museum
Courthouse and 15th Street
Silverton, CO 81433
Phone: (970) 387-5838; Winter: (970)
387-5609
www.silvertonhistoricalsociety.org

Open: Memorial Day to mid-October, 7
days/week, 9:00 A.M.–5:00 P.M. Changes
in mid-September.

Info: The museum recently received a
collection of minerals and gems from the
estate of a woman who collected in the
Silverton area for over 50 years. Highlights include quartz crystals, amethyst,
fluorite, rhodochrosite, calcite, silver,
gold, lead, galena, copper, iron pyrite.

Admission: Adults $3.50, children
under 12 free.

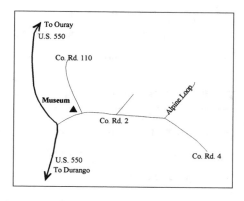

Directions: In Silverton travel north on
Main Street. The museum is next to the
courthouse and is located in the former
San Juan County Jail.

VICTOR

Mine View

Info: American Eagles Overlook. Gives a view of Colorado's largest gold mine,
the Cresson open-pit gold mine, operated by the Cripple Creek & Victor Gold
Mining Company.

TOURIST INFORMATION

State Tourist Agency

Phone: (800) COLORADO
www.colorado.com

HAWAII

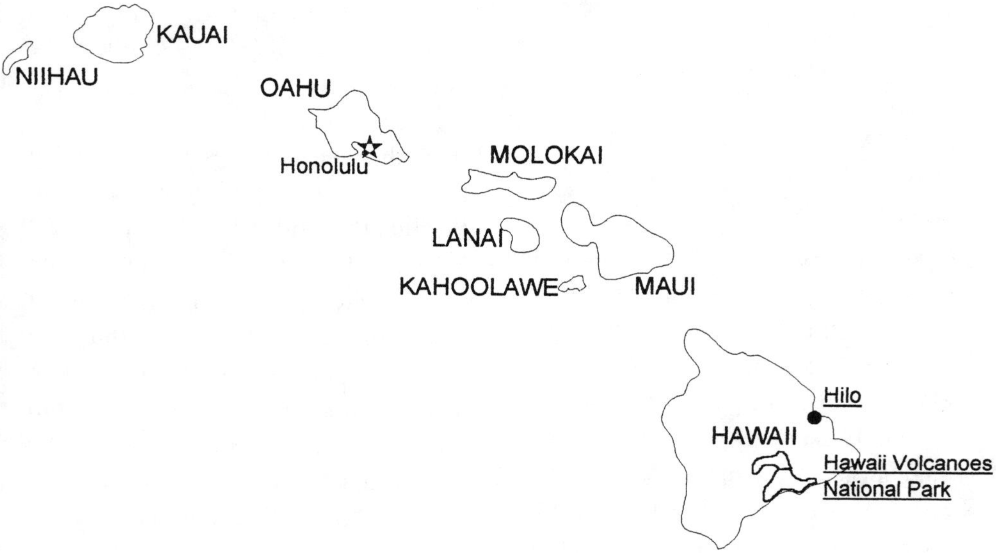

KAUAI

NIIHAU

OAHU

Honolulu

MOLOKAI

LANAI

KAHOOLAWE

MAUI

Hilo

HAWAII

Hawaii Volcanoes
National Park

State Gemstone: Black Coral

SECTION 1: Fee Dig Sites and Guide Services

No information available.

SECTION 2: Museums and Mine Tours

HAWAII NATIONAL PARK

Museum/Volcano Tour

Thomas A. Jaggar Museum
P.O. Box 52
Hawaii Volcanoes National Park
Hawaii National Park, HI 96718
Phone: (808) 985-6000

Open: All year, 8:30 A.M.–5:00 P.M., daily.
Info: Many of the gems and minerals discussed in this book were formed as a result of volcanic activity. In Hawaii, visitors can witness the power of the volcano.

The Jaggar Museum is a geological museum about vulcanology and seismology. Equipment used to detect and monitor earthquakes and eruptions is displayed, and films of past volcanic eruptions run continuously. An outlook adjacent to the museum offers views of Kilauea Caldera and Halema'uma'u Crater.

Stop at the Kilauea Visitor's Center (open 7:45 A.M.–5:00 P.M.) for an orientation to park roads, trails, activities, scenic stops, and *safety precautions:* Hawaii Volcanoes National Park is situated on two active volcanoes, and there may be hazards to the unwary and to those unfamiliar with volcanic environments.

For a recorded update on current volcanic activity, call (808) 985-6000 (24 hours).

Short walks include a 20-minute walk through a tree fern forest and a cave-like prehistoric lava tube; a 30-minute walk through the cinder outfall of the 1959 Kilauea Iki eruption; a 10-minute walk to the crater's edge of Halema'uma'u Crater; or a 2-hour hike descending 400 feet through native forest, into a crater, and across lava flows still steaming from the 1959 Kilauea Iki eruption; or a 2-hour hike over 1973–1974 lava flows to the top of a 150-foot prehistoric cinder cone.

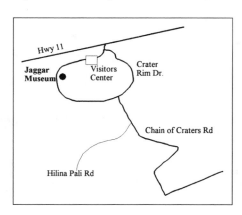

Admission: Park admission $10.00/car, good for seven days.

Directions: The Kilauea Visitor's Center and the Jaggar Museum are 30 miles from Hilo on Highway 11.

HILO

Museum

Lyman Museum
276 Haili Street
Hilo, HI 96720
Phone: (808) 935-5021
Fax: (808) 969-7685
E-mail: info@lymanmuseum.org
www.lymanmuseum.org

Open: All year, 9:30 A.M.– 4:30 P.M., Monday–Saturday.

Info: The museum's collection of rocks, minerals, gems, and fossils was primarily collected by Orlando Hammond Lyman, a great-grandson of Reverend David Belden Lyman and his wife, Sarah. The collection has been rated one of the top ten in the nation. The Lyman Museum presently exhibits the minerals in the Earth Heritage Gallery, which also has an exhibit about Hawaii before humans.

Admission: Adults $10.00, children $3.00, seniors $8.00.

Directions: Haili Street can be reached from Kamehameha Avenue, which runs along Hilo Bay. The museum is at the corner of Haili and Kapiolani Streets.

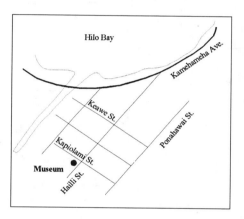

SECTION 3: Special Events and Tourist Information

TOURIST INFORMATION

State Tourist Agency

Hawaii Visitors and Convention Bureau
2270 Kalakaua Ave., Suite 801
Honolulu, HI 96815
Phone: (800) 464-2924
www.gohawaii.com

KANSAS

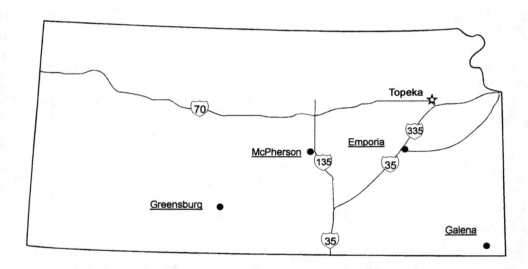

No information available.

ASHLAND

Museum 🏛

Pioneer-Krier Museum
430 W. 4th, Highway 160
P.O. Box 862
Ashland, KS 67831
Phone: (620) 635-2227
Fax: (620) 635-2227 (call first)
E-mail: pioneer@ucom.net
http://users.ucom.net/~pioneer

Open: 10:00 A.M.–5:00 P.M. Monday–Friday (closed between noon and 1:00 P.M.), closed major holidays.
Info: The museum has displays of gems and minerals.
Admission: Donations.
Directions: Call for directions.

EMPORIA

Museum 🏛

Johnston Geology Museum
Earth Science Department, Division of Physical Sciences
Emporia State University
Emporia, KS 55801
Phone: (620) 341-5330
www.emporia.edu/earthsci/museum/museum.htm

Open: When school is in session, Monday–Friday, 8:00 A.M.–10:00 P.M., Saturday 8:00 A.M.–noon
Info: Included among the displays in the museum is the Tri-State Mining Display and geological specimens, mostly from Kansas.
Admission: Free.
Directions: On the ESU campus, in Cram Science Hall at 14th and Merchant Street.

GALENA

Museum 🏛

Galena Mining & Historical Museum
319 W. 7th Street
Galena, KS 66739
Phone: (620) 783-2192

Open: Monday–Friday, 1:30 P.M.–4:30 P.M.
Info: Focuses on the local lead mining and smelting industry. Includes a collection of mining art. Galena is the oldest mining town in Kansas.
Admission: Free.

Other attractions: Big Brutus, the second-largest electric mining shovel in the world (16 stories high), is on display (for a fee) in nearby West Mineral, KS, 7 miles north and 6 miles west of Columbus, KS, on Kansas Highway 102.

GREENSBURG

Geologic Landmark: Pallasite Meteorite

Greensburg Chamber of Commerce
c/o The Big Well Museum
315 South Sycamore
Greensburg, KS 67054
Phone: (316) 723-2261; (800) 207-7369
E-mail: bigwell@midway.net
www.bigwell.org

Open: Year round; closed some holidays. Memorial Day–Labor Day, 8:00 A.M.–8:00 P.M.; Labor Day–Memorial Day, 9:00 A.M.–5:00 P.M.

Info: Frank Kimberly and his wife, Eliza, recorded a homestead claim in Kiowa County, Kansas, in February 1886. Soon Eliza found unusually heavy black rocks, which she thought were meteorites. She started writing to various colleges, trying to interest some knowledgeable person to come and examine the stones. Professor Cragin, of Washburn University, finally risked his money and time to travel to the Kimberly homestead with his farm wagon. He returned with stones that he was confident were from a rare type of meteorite, which would arouse interest in the scientific community.

In 1949, H. O. Stockwell used a modern metal detector and equipment rigged at the Peck farm to uncover the largest pallasite found to date: the Space Wanderer, weighing 1,000 pounds. Local residents wanted to keep the meteorite in the vicinity, and at the urging of a member of the Greensburg Chamber of Commerce, that organization purchased the stone. The pallasite was placed in the Greensburg Big Well Museum in 1949, where it is on display. There is a specimen weighing 740 pounds from this same meteorite shower on display at the Smithsonian Institution in Washington, DC.

Admission: Free.

Directions: U.S. 54 travels east–west through Greensburg. 315 South Sycamore Street is two blocks south of U.S. 54, at the intersection with Wisconsin Avenue.

MCPHERSON

Museum

McPherson Museum
1130 E. Euclid Street
McPherson, KS 67460
Phone: (620) 241-8464
Fax: (620) 241-8464
E-mail: mcmuseum@sbcglobal.net
www.mcphersonmuseum.org

Open: All year except holidays, 1:00–5:00 P.M., Tuesday–Sunday, or by appointment.

Info: Rocks and minerals that emphasize Kansas geology. Displays of igneous rocks, petrified wood, minerals from the United States, and a collection of speleotherms (cave features such as stalactites, stalagmites, etc.). These were collected many years ago, before it was realized that these features take hundreds, if not thousands, of years to form. The museum emphasizes that caves are fragile environments and that many states now have laws against the removal of cave features.

A small display shows the work of J. Willard Hershey, one of the first, if not *the* first, scientist to synthesize diamonds in the laboratory. Dr. Hershey was a professor at McPherson College from 1918-1943. In the 1920's, he successfully synthesized diamonds on several occasions using a high temperature furnace, molten lead, and sugar carbon. A specimen of his synthesized diamonds is on display as well as some papers and pictures.

Approximately 35 meteorites are on exhibit, collected by representatives of McPherson College. Many of the meteorites on display were collected in Kansas; others were collected from Iowa, Colorado, New Mexico, Arizona, Nebraska, Texas, and Mexico.

One interesting story included on file is of a stony meteorite that fell on November 9, 1923, near Coldwater, Kansas. It was witnessed by many people throughout Kansas, Oklahoma, and New Mexico. Having witnessed it from McPherson, H. H. Nininger set about the task of locating its fall. After corresponding with about 100 people scattered over three states, he finally determined that a piece of it had fallen near Coldwater. Almost a year later, this mass, weighing 11 pounds, was plowed from a field near Coldwater. It was donated to the museum by H. H. Nininger.

Admission: Free; donation requested.

Directions: McPherson is located just west of I-135, on U.S. 56.

SECTION 3: Special Events and Tourist Information

TOURIST INFORMATION

State Tourist Agency ☞

Division of Travel & Tourism
1000 SW Jackson Street, Suite 100
Topeka, KS 66612
Phone: (785) 296-2009
http://www.kansascommerce.com

NEVADA

State Gemstone: Virgin Valley Black Fire Opal (1987) (Precious);
Nevada Turquoise (1987) (Semiprecious)
State Mineral: Silver
State Stone/Rock: Sandstone (1987)

DENIO

Dig for Opal *T*

The following gems or minerals may be found:

- Fire wood opal

Summer: May 25–September 30
Bonanza Opal Mines, Inc.
P.O. Box 121
Denio, NV 89404
Phone: (775) 941-0121

Winter: October 1–May 24
Bonanza Opal Mines, Inc.
62550 Waugh Road
Bend, OR 97701
Phone: (541) 383-1700

E-mail: nadine1700@aol.com
www.goldnuggetwebs.com/bonanza

Open: 8:00 A.M.–4:00 P.M., Memorial Day weekend–September 30.
Info: The Bonanza was first mined in 1905.
Other services available: Free campground with showers.
Admission: Adults $40.00 per day, children under 12 free.
Directions: From Lakeview, OR, travel 85 miles east on Highway 140. At that point, you will pass a rest area on the right; drive ½ mile further and turn right onto a dirt road. You will pass a campground; 4½ miles after the campground,

---

High Desert Opal Mines of Western Nevada

Virgin Valley opal is wood opal. It was formed as the result of silica filling the cavities in, or left by, logs, branches, or twigs from ancient forests buried by volcanic ash some 15–25 million years ago. Virgin Valley is famous for black opal. Specimens of black opal from the Rainbow Ridge Mine are on display at the Smithsonian Institution in Washington, D.C.

Opal at the Royal Rainbow Mine is nothing like that found in Virgin Valley mines just a few miles to the north. The opal here is found in hard black basalt filled with vugs, or openings left by gas bubbles trapped as the molten rock solidified. Some of the vugs are filled with opal, mostly clear to opaque, with an orange base similar to opal from Mexico. Associated with the precious opal are common orange jelly opal and fire opal.

Note: Opal hunting in the High Desert of Nevada is hard work, but the reward can be a find of beautiful opal, and the scenery is breathtaking. In addition, one may see eagles, wild mustangs, and other wildlife.

turn right at the Bonanza sign, then drive 1 mile to the mine. From Winnemucca, NV, take Highway 95 north for 35 miles to Highway 140, and turn left to Denio Junction. At Denio Junction, Highway 140 will turn left again; drive 25 miles to the graded dirt road to the campground.

DENIO

Dig for Opal T

The following gems or minerals may be found:
- **Crystal, white, and black fire opal**

The Opal Queen Mining Company
Denio, NV 89404
Phone: (775) 941-0130

Lenny Marley
421 Santa Clara Avenue
Alameda, CA 94501
Phone: (510) 205-1860
E-mail: opallenny@aol.com
www.opalqueen.com

Info: Until recently, the mine was not open to the public; however, the owners have started private digs on a reservation only basis, when the weather permits. The reservations are for a single party of 4 persons per day.
Admission: $1,000.00 per party of 4 per day; must reserve 4 days. FOR SERIOUS DIGGERS ONLY!
Directions: Directions will be provided with the reservation confirmation.

DENIO/ *Native • Moderate to Difficult*

Tailings Digging for Opal T

The following gems or minerals may be found:
- **Opal, wood-opal**

Rainbow Ridge Opal Mine
Glen and Donna Hodson
Box 97
Denio, NV 89404
Phone: (775) 941-0270 (Memorial Day–Labor Day); (541) 548-4810 (rest of year)
E-mail: glen@nevadaopal.com
www.nevadaopal.com
Winter:
437 NW 7th Street
Redmond, OR 97756
E-mail: glen@nevadaopal.com

Open: Friday of Memorial Day weekend until Labor Day Monday, 8:00 A.M.–4:00 P.M. Rock shop open until 5:00 P.M. Closed Wednesday.
Info: Wood-opal combinations can be found in mine tailings (the material left over during mining operations) that are 7–8 feet deep. Find opal that came as

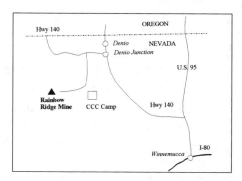

casts after wood. Lots of wood-opal combinations can be found. Visit the shop before digging, as it will help you to know what you are looking for. The owners say that what you will find is determined in part by luck, but mostly by knowing what you are hunting for, and how to hunt.

Bring your own tools. Suggested tools include a small garden rake, a small shovel or trowel, a spray bottle for water, and a large bucket for opal. You may also want to bring a hat and sunblock, and gloves.

Admission: $40.00/day, keep all you find. Children 10–15 half rate; children under 10 free when accompanying an adult.

The mine is currently offering, based on limited availability, virgin ground digging. The mine will bring out a bucket of virgin soil from the mine, approximately 3 cubic yards, and one or two people (plus children) may search that load all day. The fee is $300.00/load/day (5 day max). Reservations only, which also allows tailings digging after you've finished the bucket load. The soil will be newly mined opal clay, and there is no guarantee as to its contents; however, you keep whatever you find. Call for more information or to make arrangements for this offering.

Other services available: Small rock shop at mine; restrooms. There is no overnight camping. Trailers should be left at the CCC Camp, which is 5 miles from the mine. Camping at the CCC Camp is free, and it has water, toilets, and a swimming pool.

Directions: From Denio Junction, take Route 140 toward Lakeview, OR. At 24½ miles, turn left onto a dirt road to the mine. The CCC Camp is 2½ miles from Route 140; the mine is 5 miles beyond the CCC Camp. There are signs from the CCC Camp to Rainbow Ridge Mine.

Note: The closest town is Denio Junction, some 33 miles from the mine. The last 7½ miles to the mine is dirt and gravel. During wet weather, the last couple of miles can be very bad and should not be attempted. Call ahead for weather information.

DENIO / *Native ▪ Moderate to Difficult*

Dig Your Own
Black Opal and Fire Opal *T*

The following gems or minerals may be found:

▪ **Black opal, fire opal**

Royal Peacock Opal Mine, Inc.
Joy and Harry Wilson
P.O. Box 165
Denio, NV 89404
Phone: (775) 941-0374 (mine)

Open: 7 days/week, weather permitting. May 15–October 15, 8:00 A.M.– 4:00 P.M. Rock Shop 8:00 A.M.– 5:00 P.M.

Info: Opal hunters here have two options. One is to dig into the bank of undisturbed montmorillonite where the opals are found. The second and easier option is to dig in the tailings. Bring your own tools. No rock hammers are

Garnets may be found in two different ways. The first involves searching the surface and drainage ways for the dark-colored stones, which have weathered from the volcanic rock (rhyolite). The garnets are washed downhill and collect in pockets, much like a gold placer deposit. Canyons and drainageways downhill from the garnet field are likely places to search.

The second way is harder but sometimes more rewarding. This method is to break the garnet-bearing rock with a hammer or pick to reveal the gems. The garnets usually occur as single crystals attached to small cavities, called vugs or vesicles, within the rock. When searching for source rocks, look for material that has veins or cavities lined with quartz. Carefully break the rock to see what is inside. If a garnet is found, it can be left in the rock or removed by carefully picking it out with a stout pocket knife or similar tool.

permitted. Suggested tools include a screwdriver; a small shovel; a pick, garden rake, or trowel; a 2½-pound pick with a very sharp point for digging into clay; a spray bottle for water; and a small bucket. You may want to bring gloves, a hat, sunscreen, and a kneeling pad. Visit the shop before digging, as it will help you to know what you are looking for.

Bank digging: $110.00/day/person; keep all you find. Tailings digging: $45.00/day/person; keep all you find.

Other services available: Small rock shop at mine with specimen opals, tools, and supplies; restrooms; public phone. *Note:* The closest town is Denio Junction, 33 miles from the mine.

Campground rates: $5.00/day/person, $20.00 per RV with hookups (reservations suggested), $50.00 per day for furnished trailer (one available—reservations required), $5.00 per use for shower room. Laundry room available.

Directions: From Denio Junction, take Route 140 toward Lakeview, OR. At 24½ miles, turn left onto a dirt road to the mine; follow the signs to the Virgin Valley Ranch and mines. A CCC Campground (available for public camping) is 2½ miles from Route 140.

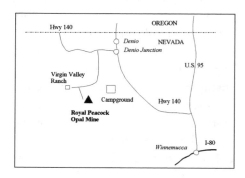

ELY / *Native • Easy to Difficult*

Search or Dig for Garnets 𝑇

The following gems or minerals may be found:

- Dark red almandine garnets

Garnet Fields Rockhound Area
Ely Bureau of Land Management District
White Pine Chamber of Commerce
636 Aultman St.
Ely, NV 89301
Phone: (775) 289-8877
Fax: (775) 289-6144
E-mail: elyce@idsely.com
www.elynevada.net

Open: Daily.

Info: Search in a 1,280-acre area of public land for dark red almandine garnets found in volcanic rock. Locally referred to as Garnet Hill, this nationally known rockhounding area is famous for its dark red garnets in volcanic rock.

Bring your own tools. Suggested tools include a hammer, a small shovel or trowel, a screwdriver, and a bucket for your finds. You may also want to bring a hat and sunblock, and gloves.

Admission: Free.

Other services available: Limited camping space for tents or small RVs, picnic tables, group campfire area, restrooms (including wheelchair-accessible toilet).

Info: Garnet Hill is one of the better

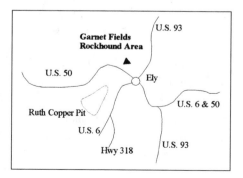

areas from which to view the large open-pit copper mine and multihued waste rock dumps in the nearby Robinson Mining District.

Directions: Garnet Fields Rockhound Area is located on U.S. 50 about 6½ miles west of the traffic signal at the U.S. 93/U.S. 50 junction in Ely.

RENO / *Native • Easy to Difficult*

Dig for Gems and Minerals *T*

The following gems or minerals may be found:

- Amethyst, smoky quartz, turquoise, variscite, Mt. Ariy blue chalcedony, Virgin Valley opal, fire opal, plume agate, and sunstones

High Desert Gems & Minerals
Phone: (775) 772-7724 (Phone sometimes not in network, so keep trying.)
E-mail: tourmalineminer@aol.com
www.highdesertgemsandminerals.com

Open: In the spring, by reservation only.

Info: This is a five-day gem mine tour, usually for 2–6 people at a time, going to a different mine each day. Transportation is provided, but bring your own camping gear.

Fees: $1200.00/person.

Directions: Get directions when you make your reservation.

LAS VEGAS

Museum 🏛

Nevada State Museum and Historical Society
700 Twin Lakes Drive
Las Vegas, NV 89107
Phone: (702) 486-5205
Fax: (702) 486-5172

Open: Daily, 9:00 A.M.–5:00 P.M.; closed for major holidays.

Info: The museum has exhibits that advance the understanding of the history, pre-history, and natural history of Nevada.

Admission: Adults $4.00, seniors $3.00, children under 18 free.

Directions: The museum is located in Lorenzi Park, overlooking the Lake.

RENO

Museum 🏛

W.M. Keck Earth Science and Mineral Engineering Museum
Mackay School of Mines
University of Nevada
Reno, NV 89501
Phone: (702) 784-6052
E-mail: rdolbier@unr.edu
http://mines.unr.edu/museum

Open: 9:00 A.M.–4:00 P.M., Monday–Friday, closed weekends and school holidays.

Info: The museum has an outstanding collection of minerals, ores, photographs, and mining-related relics. There is an emphasis on early Nevada mining history. There are samples from famous mining districts, such as Comstock, Tonopah, and Goldfield.

Admission: Free.

Directions: Located in the Mackay School of Mines Building. Parking available near the Center Street entrance to the University.

VIRGINIA CITY

Mine Tour 🏛

Chollar Mine
South F Street
Virginia City, NV 89440
Phone: (775) 847-0155

Open: March–September. March–mid-June (weather permitting): Monday–Thursday, 1:00–4:00 P.M.; mid-June–September, 7 days/week, 12:00–5:00 P.M.

Info: Experience this underground tour in the last of the Comstock ore body's old original gold and silver mines. See square-set timbering, ore, old tools, and equipment. Of the 50 mines in the Comstock, the Chollar Mine was the fifth highest in production, earning $17 million.

Admission: Adults $4.50, children (4–14) $1.00.

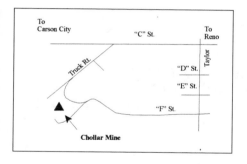

Directions: On south F Street, in Virginia City.

SECTION 3: Special Events and Tourist Information

TOURIST INFORMATION

State Tourist Agency ☞

Nevada Commission on Tourism
401 N. Carson Street
Carson City, NV 89701
Phone: (800) NEVADA 8 (638-2328)
www.travelnevada.com

NEW MEXICO

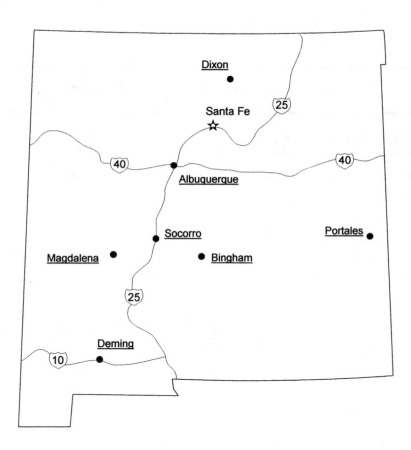

State Gemstone: Turquoise (1967)

BINGHAM / *Native • Easy, Moderate to Difficult*

Collect as Many as 84 Different Minerals at Old Mines *T*

The following gems or minerals may be found:

• Quartz, barite, fluorite, galena, selenite, linarite, brochantite, *amethyst,* wulfenite, calcite, *spangolite,* aurichalcite, cerussite, *covelite,* jarosite, *smithsonite, chrysocolla,* hemimorphite, *murdochite, plattnerite,* and *cuprite.* (Minerals in italics found through guided tours only.)

Hansonborg Mining District
Blanchard Rock Shop
2972 Highway 380
Bingham, NM 87832
Phone: (505) 423-3235
E-mail: blanchardrock@plateautel.net
www.blanchardrockshop.com

Open: Daily, daylight to dark most of the time; please call before coming.
Info: The district includes several mining claims. The Desert Rose is the only claim open for public collecting. There are other claims that can be visited through guided tours. Please contact the rock shop owner(s) for more information on collecting or going on a tour.

The first lead mine was opened by Western Mineral Products in 1916. Mr. F. L. Blanchard took over the mines in 1943. Several mining ventures occurred subsequently; however, all buildings have been removed, and the mines are now operated exclusively for rockhounds.
Admission: Call shop for rates.
Other services available: Rock shop, guided tours throughout the state.
Directions: From Albuquerque, take I-25 south to the San Antonio exit. Drive east on Highway 380 for 30 miles, and look for the rock shop sign.

DEMING / *Native • Moderate to Difficult*

Collect Up to 15 Pounds of Semiprecious Stones *T*

The following gems or minerals may be found:

• Silica minerals; quartz crystals; chalcedony; agate (blue); common opal (white-pink); jasper (yellow, pink, orange, brown, chocolate, and variegated nodules); thundereggs; geodes filled with either agate or common opal or both, or hollow, lined with chalcedony or quartz crystals; manganese oxide minerals; gray to black perlite; pitch stone, some with seams of red and brown; and manganese minerals

Rockhound State Park
P.O. Box 1064
Deming, NM 88030
Phone: (505) 546-6182

Open: All year; gates locked at sundown to 7:30 A.M.

Info: The park is located on the western slope of the Little Florida Mountains, which is an extrusive formation made mostly of volcanic mud called rhyolite. 15 pounds of rock per person may be collected from the park. Bring your own tools (rock hammer, small shovel, canvas bag) and drinking water container.

Admission: $5.00/day.

Other services available: Visitors center with geological rock display, water and botanical gardens, and hiking.

Campground: RV and tent sites, some with electricity (14-day camping limit); restrooms; showers; dump station; self-pay service station; group shelter; camping reservations available.

Rates: Call for rates.

Directions: From Deming, take NM 11 south five miles, turn east on Rockhound Road—about 8 miles to park.

DIXON / *Native • Moderate to Difficult*

Look for Over 50 Different Minerals *T*

The following gems or minerals may be found:

• Quartz, beryl, garnet, microlite, apatite, clevelandite, spodumene, spessartine, albite, muscovite, lepidolite, and others

Harding Mine
c/o Department of Earth and Planetary Sciences
Nothrop Hall

University of New Mexico
Albuquerque, NM 87131-1116
Phone: (505) 277-4204
Fax: (505) 277-8843

Open: 8:00 A.M.–5:00 P.M.

Info: Collecting is restricted to material for personal collections (approximately 5 pounds/person). The Harding mine has yielded commercial quantities of beryl, lepidolite, spodumene, and microlite over half a century. It is also a classic locality for scientific studies of pegmatites.

Because pegmatite magmas are volatile fractions, they host a unique and unusual collection of elements. The conditions of crystallization allow these elements to form minerals that are gigantic in size. The Harding is famous as the world's largest deposit of microlite (a complex tantalum oxide). About 50 minerals occur in the main dike. This number is not astounding; some pegmatites in New England have over 100 different mineral species. (See listing under Ruggles Mine in New Hampshire.)

Note: Permission to visit the Harding mine must be obtained from the Department of Earth and Planetary Sciences (http://epswww.unm.edu/harding/release/relform.htm) or from the mine caretaker, Gilbert Griego. A release must be signed at Gilbert Griego's residence.

Visitors are not permitted to enter any of the underground workings. Children must be supervised individually by an adult.

Admission: Free; must sign an acknowledgment of risk form. Donations are

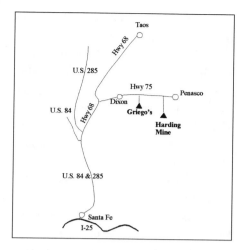

MAGDALENA / *Native ▪ Moderate to Difficult*

Collect Copper and Iron Minerals on Mine Dumps *T*

The following gems or minerals may be found:

▪ Hematite, pyrite, azurite, malachite, smithsonite, hedenburgite, aurichalcite, other iron and copper minerals

Bill's Gems and Minerals
Helen Dobson
P.O. Box 141
Magdalena, NM 87825
Phone: (505) 854-2236

Open: Call to make arrangements and for information about hours.
Admission: $5.00/day; collect up to 20 pounds/day. Call for weather and road conditions and to be sure the collecting area is open. Road requires a high-clearance vehicle.
Directions: From Albuquerque, take I-25 south to U.S. 60. Exit onto U.S. 60 west, and drive 27 miles to Magdalena.

appreciated. Groups of 10 or more are required to pay $50.00
Directions: From I-25, take U.S. 285 north, then take State Highway 68 toward Taos. Take State Highway 75 east from Highway 68 through Dixon toward Penasco. 1.2 miles after passing Zeller's Store in Dixon, turn right on County Road 63 to get to the residence of Gilbert Griego to sign the release. Return to Highway 75 and drive 5.3 miles farther to get to the mine.

SECTION 2: Museums and Mine Tours

ALBUQUERQUE

Museum
Silver Family Geology Museum
University of New Mexico
Albuquerque, NM 87131
Phone: (505) 277-4204

Fax: (505) 277-8843
Open: Monday–Friday, 7:30 A.M.–4:30 P.M.
Info: Exhibits at the museum include New Mexico minerals, fossils, gemstones and their uses, minerals used in everyday life, and several on the geology of features

unique to New Mexico. A fluorescent mineral display is located in an adjacent room.

Admission: Free.

Directions: The museum is located on the first floor of Northrop Hall on the UNM campus, on the west side of the Yale pedestrian mall, a block north of Central Avenue.

ALBUQUERQUE

Museum

Institute of Meteoritics
200 Yale NE
The University of New Mexico
Albuquerque, NM 87131-1126
Phone: (505) 277-1644
Fax: (505) 277-3577
http://epswww.unm.edu/

Open: Monday–Friday, 9:00 A.M.–4:00 P.M.

Info: The institute was founded in 1944 and is devoted to research and teaching in the field of meteoritics and planetary sciences. It houses an extensive collection of

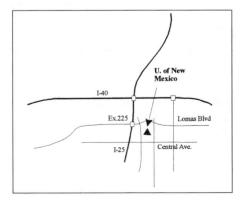

meteorites, recovered in New Mexico and around the world.

Meteorites are solid pieces of material that have fallen to earth from space. Most are thought to have come from the asteroid belt; however, a few may have come from the moon or from Mars. Meteorites are therefore valuable from a scientific standpoint because they are samples of many different planetary bodies in our solar system.

Visitors to the Museum can see examples of the various types of meteorites:

• Achondrites are stony meteorites containing 0% to 30% metal, with no silicate spheres.

• Chondrites contain 0% to 30% metal and millimeter-sized silicate spheres called chondrules. The chondrites, which are the most common meteorites, are significant because they formed at the same time as the solar system, 4.6 billion years ago.

• Pallasites are composed of 50% metal and 50% rounded crystals of a mineral called olivine.

• Mesosiderites are composed of 50% metal and 50% angular rock fragments.

• Iron meteorites, composed of nearly 100% metal, are placed in one of three classifications—octahedrites, hexahedrites, or ataxites—depending on the structure of the metal crystals inside.

Admission: Free.

Directions: The institute is located on the campus of the University of New Mexico. The campus can be reached by taking the Lomas Boulevard exit off I-25, and driving east.

ALBUQUERQUE

Museum 🏛

New Mexico Museum of Natural
History and Science
1801 Mountain Road N.W.
Albuquerque, NM 87104
Phone: (505) 841-2800
Fax: (505) 841-8866
www.nmnaturalhistory.org

Open: Daily, except Christmas, Thanksgiving and nonholiday Mondays in January and September, 9:00 A.M.–5:00 P.M.
Info: The mineral collection consists of approximately 3,000 specimens, with a focus on New Mexico and the southwest United States.
Admission: Adults $6.00, seniors $5.00, children (3–12) $3.00.
Other services available: Dynatheater, gift shop, restaurant.
Directions: From I-40, take Rio Grande Boulevard south about ½ a mile to Mountain Road, then east on Mountain Road less than ½ a mile to the museum, turning north on 18th Street to the parking lot. The Museum entrance is on 18th Street.

ALBUQUERQUE

Museum 🏛

The Turquoise Museum
2107 Central N.W.
Albuquerque, NM 87104
Phone: (505) 247-8650

Open: Monday–Saturday, 9:30 A.M.–4:00 P.M. Personal tours and group arrangements can be made by calling ahead.
Info: This museum is privately owned and devoted to the story of turquoise. On display is natural turquoise from active and historical sites around the world. Also displayed are various materials that have been created to lower the cost and/or improve the appearance of less valuable stones. It is estimated that only about 10% of the turquoise on the market today is real, natural turquoise. One of the museum's major aims is to educate consumers so they can better determine exactly what they want and how to protect themselves in the marketplace.
Admission: Adults $4.00, seniors and AAA $3.00, children under 18 $3.00.

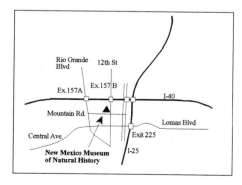

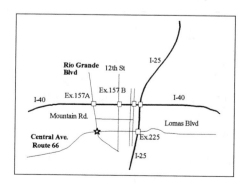

Other services: Gift shop.

Directions: The museum is located on Central Avenue (Route 66) near its intersection with Rio Grande Boulevard, ¼ block west of Old Town Plaza, next to Walgreens.

PORTALES

Museum

Miles Mineral Museum
Roosevelt Hall
Eastern New Mexico University
1200 W. University
Portales, NM 88130
Phone: (505) 562-2651
www.enmu.edu/academics/excellence/
museums/miles-mineral

Open: Monday–Friday, 8:00 A.M.–5:00 P.M.; Saturday by appointment.
Info: Displays minerals, gems, and meteorites.
Admission: Free.
Direction: Call for directions.

SOCORRO

Museum

Mineralogical Museum
200W - Workman Addition
New Mexico Tech Campus
Socorro, NM 87801
Phone: (505) 835-5420

Open: All year, 8:00 A.M.–5:00 P.M., Monday–Friday. 10:00 A.M.–3:00 P.M.

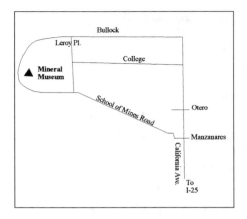

Saturday and Sunday. Special arrangements for groups at other times must be made in writing.

Info: Begun as the mineral collection of the Geology Department of the New Mexico School of Mines, the museum collection now contains more than 10,000 specimens. The collection is in four sections: the display collection, the reserve collection, the reference collection, and the micromount collection. The extensive collection on display is subdivided into six sections:

The New Mexico section contains minerals collected within the state.

Another section is devoted to minerals from other states, including New Jersey; the Tri-State District of Missouri, Oklahoma, and Kansas; and Arizona.

The third section contains minerals from 35 foreign countries. Noteworthy specimens are from Mont St. Hilaire, Quebec, Canada; Tsumeb, Namibia; England; Japan; and Mexico.

The fourth section contains fluorescent minerals, including specimens from

Franklin, NJ, and from New Mexico.

The fifth section contains fossils.

The sixth section is the Dana reference collection, where minerals are presented as classified by the Dana system. This display exhibits 475 minerals representing 475 species. The minerals in this display are not always well-crystallized beautiful specimens, but rather the more common, massive varieties that would likely be found by prospectors and rockhounds. Prospectors often study the Dana display to determine the appearance of the ore minerals for which they are searching.

Also on display in the museum are minerals offered for sale. Museum personnel actively collect, buy, and trade mineral specimens to add to the collection. The museum maintains a set of New Mexico specimens for sale. Specimens from other localities are also sold, and trading is welcomed.

A mineralogist/museum curator will identify minerals and rocks as a service to the public.

Admission: Free.

Directions: From I-25, take California Avenue north to Manzanares. Turn left on Manzanares to Socorro Plaza, and turn right on School of Mines Road. Follow that to the museum.

SECTION 3: Special Events and Tourist Information

ANNUAL EVENT

New Mexico Mineral Symposium, Socorro, NM

Info: The Symposium, held for two days in November, includes lectures, exhibits, and displays. Several mineral localities are available for field collecting via self-guided tours.

For registration or more information on the Symposium contact:
New Mexico Institute of Mining & Technology
Socorro, NM 87801
www.geoinfo.nmt.edu/about/home.html

TOURIST INFORMATION

State Tourist Agency

New Mexico Department of Tourism
491 Old Santa Fe Trail
Santa Fe, NM 87501
Phone: (800) SEE NEW MEX (733-6396) ext. 0643
www.newmexico.org

OKLAHOMA

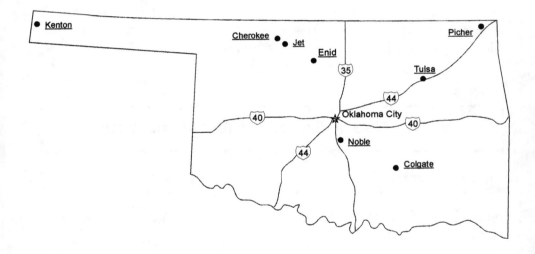

State Stone/Rock: Barite Rose

JET / *Native • Easy to Moderate*

Dig for Selenite Crystals *T*

The following gems or minerals may be found:

• **Selenite crystals**

Salt Plains National Wildlife Refuge
Department of the Interior, US Fish and
Wildlife Service
Route 1, Box 76
Jet, OK 73749
Phone: (580) 626-4794

Open: Daily, 7 days/week, sunrise to sunset. April 1–October 15.

Info: Find single crystals, penetration twins, and crystal clusters. Soil, sand, and/or clay particles in the crystals often form an hourglass shape found only in this area. Other foreign objects in the soil such as sticks, rocks, and even cockleburs are sometimes included in the crystals.

The salt plains, a flat expanse of mud completely devoid of vegetation, are located in north central Oklahoma. The surface of the plains is covered by a thin layer of salt. The plains, 7 miles in length and approximately 3 miles wide, lie in the Salt Plains National Wildlife Refuge, an important feeding and resting area for migratory waterfowl and endangered species.

No permit is required. Collectors may remove up to 10 pounds of crystals

What Is Selenite?

Selenite is a crystallized form of gypsum, which is a hydrous calcium sulfate. Gypsum, a common mineral, can take on a great variety of crystal forms and shapes. On the Salt Plains, the crystals form just below the salt-encrusted surface and are seldom found deeper than 2 feet.

The crystals take on the characteristics of their environment: the finer the soil, the clearer the crystals. Iron oxide in the soil gives the crystals their chocolate brown color. Sand and clay particles from the surrounding soil are often included within the crystals. These particles often form an hourglass shape, found only in this area. Exceptional individual crystals measuring up to 7 inches long have been found, as have complex combinations weighing as much as 38 pounds.

Collecting Selenite Crystals

- Use a shovel and dig a hole about 2 feet across and at least 2 feet deep, or deep enough to reach wet sand.
- Allow 2–3 inches of water to seep in from the bottom.
- Splash water gently around the

sides of the hole. When you uncover crystals, continue splashing to wash the crystals out.
- Be careful when removing the crystals, since they will be wet and fragile.

plus one large cluster for their personal use in any one day.

Bring your own equipment: a shovel, a container such as a jug or bucket filled with water, a blanket or sheet to work on, and a container to store fragile crystals.

Because of the white salt surface, it is easy to get sunburned. Sunglasses and protective clothing are recommended.

Admission: Free.

Other services available: Cabins, campsites, and RV sites are available at the Great Salt Plains State Park.

Directions: To reach the gate leading into the crystal digging area, go 6 miles

west of Jet on U.S. 64, then go north on a dirt road for 3 miles, and then east 1 mile to the gate. From Cherokee, go 3 miles south from Fifth Street in Cherokee on U.S. 64, then go east 6 miles on a paved road to the gate.

KENTON / *Native • Moderate to Difficult*

Rockhounding on a Working Cattle Ranch *T*

The following gems or minerals may be found:

- **Agate, jasper, and petrified wood**

Black Mesa Bed & Breakfast
Monty Joe and Vicki Roberts
P.O. Box 81
Kenton, OK 73946
Phone: (580) 261-7443; (800) 821-7204

Open: Call to make arrangements for your visit.

Info: Bring your own equipment.

Rates: $1.00/pound for agate, jasper, and petrified wood; $10.00/pound for cycads

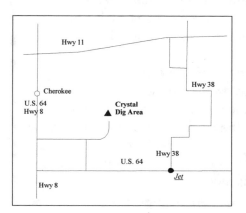

and $10.00/pound for "copelite."

Other services available: The Black Mesa Bed & Breakfast in the Dry Cimmaron Valley in the northwest corner of the Oklahoma panhandle is located just 2 miles north of Kenton, near the base of the magnificent Black Mesa. Accommodation in the 1910 native rock ranch house includes a second story suite that sleeps six, and a ground-level double occupancy room. Children are welcome. Black Mesa State Park, about 9 miles from the ranch, has hookups for campers and camping. Other activities available in the area include hiking, history, fishing, hunting, and birding.

Directions: Kenton is on State Highway 325, in the Oklahoma panhandle, just a few miles east from the New Mexico border, and near the northern state border with Colorado. Black Mesa Bed & Breakfast is 2 miles north of Kenton on a local highway leading to Black Mesa.

KENTON / *Native • Moderate to Difficult*

Rockhounding on a Working Cattle Ranch *T*

The following gems or minerals may be found:

▪ **Agate, fossils**

Howard Layton
Colorado Rt.
Kenton, OK 73946
Phone: (719) 461-7457

Open: Call to make arrangements for your visit.

Info: Reports are that the West Carrizo Creek on Mr. Layton's Ranch flooded in 1998 and brought up a lot of agate and other stones. Bring your own equipment. You will need four-wheel drive or a good pair of boots for access to the collecting sites.

Admission: $0.10/pound for most agate; up to $1.00/pound for high-quality agate.

Other services available: Motor homes and campers can stay at the ranch. Mr. Layton will hook up a water hose and electricity. Other options include Camp Billie Joe, 1 mile southest of Kenton, (580) 261-7482 or 261-7424; and a bed & breakfast 3 miles north of Kenton, (580) 261-7445.

Directions: Mr. Layton's ranch is 12 miles north of Kenton, just over the Colorado state line. Call for directions.

COALGATE

Museum

Coal Country Mining & Historical Museum
212 S. Broadway
Coalgate, OK 74538
Phone: (405) 927-2360

Open: Hours vary; call ahead.
Info: A tribute to the area's mining heritage.
Admission: Donation.
Directions: Coalgate is located at the intersection of U.S. Highway 75 State Highway 3 and State Highway 43.

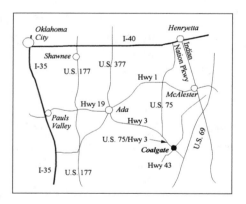

ENID

Museum

The Mr. & Mrs. Dan Midgley Museum
1001 Sequoyah Drive
Enid, OK 73073

Phone: (580) 234-7265; (580) 234-8252
Open: Tuesday–Friday 10:00 A.M.–5:00 P.M., Saturday–Sunday 1:00–5:00 P.M. Winter hours: November 1–March 31, Wednesday–Saturday, 1:00–5:00 P.M. Closed holidays.
Info: The museum is a monument to the Midgley family, one of Oklahoma's earliest landholders and most prosperous farmers. During their extensive travels to sell their harvests, they collected rocks. Carefully identified rocks from various areas of the U.S. are displayed, but the predominant areas from which rocks were collected are Oklahoma and the Texas shoreline. The collection includes over 30 types of exotic rocks, crystal agate, sandstone, and petrified wood.
Admission: Free.
Directions: Corner of Owen K. Gerriot (Highway 412) and Van Buren (U.S. 81) in Enid.

NOBLE

Museum

Timberlake Rose Rock Museum
Joe and Nancy Stine
P.O. Box 663, 419 S. Highway 77
Noble, OK 73068-0663
Phone: (405) 872-9838
www.roserockmuseum.com
Open: All year, Tuesday–Friday

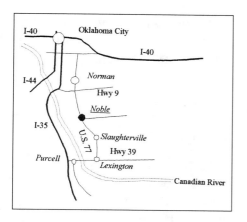

Rose rock

10:00 A.M.–6:00 P.M., Saturday 10:00 A.M.– 4:00 P.M.

Info: The museum was opened in 1986 by Joe and Nancy Stine in Noble, the "rose rock capital" of Oklahoma. Joe and Nancy create rose rock sculptures. Recipients of their artwork include Queen Elizabeth II, and their sculptures have been distributed all over the world. Beautiful rose rock clusters are displayed at the museum, and rose rock gifts may be purchased at the museum gift shop. **Admission:** Free.

Cherokee Rose Legend

In the 1800s, despite a decision in favor of the Cherokees by the U.S. Supreme Court, President Andrew Jackson ordered the removal of the Cherokees and other Indian tribes from their eastern homelands to Oklahoma, a journey later referred to as the Trail of Tears. Thousands died along the way.

Indian folklore states that God, looking down from heaven, decided to commemorate the courageous Cherokees. As the blood of the braves and the tears of the maidens fell to the ground, they were turned to stones in the shape of a rose. The rose rock is found in Oklahoma, the end of the journey. The state flower of Georgia, the tribe's eastern home, is the Cherokee rose. The Oklahoma rose rock is concentrated in central Oklahoma along an 80-mile narrow band extending from Pails Valley to Guthrie.

(Story courtesy of the Timberlake Rose Rock Museum)

Directions: The museum is located on the south side of Noble on Highway 77. The highway is also Main Street in Noble. From Oklahoma City, take I-35 south to Norman, exit onto Highway 9 east, then exit off 9 onto Highway 77, and go south 3 miles to Noble. Traveling from Dallas, exit off I-35 at Purcell and take Highway 77 north to Noble.

PICHER

Museum

Picher Mining Museum
526 N. Connell
Picher, OK 74360
Phone: (918) 673-1192

Open: May–September by appointment.
Info: History of the largest lead and zinc mining field in the world.
Admission: Free.

Directions: Picher is on U.S. 69, near the point where Oklahoma, Kansas, and Missouri meet.

TULSA

Museum

Elsing Museum
7777 S. Lewis
Tulsa, OK 74171
Phone: (918) 495-6262

Open: Wednesday–Saturday 1:30–4:30 P.M. Closed major holidays, and between Christmas and New Year's Day.
Info: 60-year collection of rare and beautiful gems and minerals.
Admission: Free.
Directions: From I-44, take south exit. Drive 3 miles south to campus of Oral Roberts University. Located on first floor of Learning Resources Center.

SECTION 3: Special Events and Tourist Information

ANNUAL EVENT

The Crystal Festival, Cherokee, OK, one Saturday in late April or Early May ☜

Features a selenite crystals digging contest with cash prizes awarded for best examples of crystals unearthed during the day. People are available to teach beginners how to find the crystals.

Other services available:
At the site: refreshments, T-shirts, and information on crystals.
In town: flea market booths and sidewalk sale, quilt show, musical entertainment, garage sale, crystal bingo, and carnival.
Directions: To reach the gate leading into the crystal digging area, go 6 miles

Selenite crystal

west of Jet, on U.S. 64, then go north on a dirt road for 3 miles, and then east 1 mile to the gate.

From Cherokee, go 3 miles south from Fifth Street in Cherokee on U.S. 64, then go east 6 miles on a paved road to the gate.

For information on crystal digging and a map of the National Wildlife Refuge, see the entry on Salt Plains National Wildlife Refuge in Section 1.

For more information contact the Cherokee Chamber of Commerce at (580) 596-3053, between 9:00 A.M. and noon, or visit www.greatsaltplains.com/events.htm.

TOURIST INFORMATION

State Tourist Agency

Oklahoma Tourism & Recreation Department
Travel & Tourism Division
P.O. Box 52002
Oklahoma City, OK 73152
Phone: (800) 652-6552; (405) 230-8400
E-mail: information@travelok.com
www.travelok.com

TEXAS

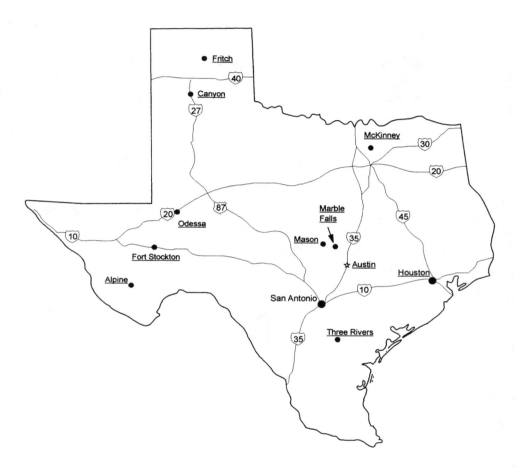

State Gemstone: Texas Blue Topaz (1969)
State Gemstone Cut: Lone Star Cut (1977)
State Stone/Rock: Petrified Palmwood (1960)

ALPINE / *Native • Difficult*

Hunt for Agate and Jasper 𝑇

The following gems or minerals may be found:

▪ Moss agate, jasper, petrified wood, occasionally banded agate or palm wood

Stillwell Ranch
HC 65, Box 430
Alpine, TX 79830
Phone: (915) 376-2244

Open: All year.

Info: The best time for rock hunting is spring or fall; summer is too hot and snake activity is greater. Avoid the second week in March—this is spring break, and the ranch is usually full.

Admission: Free; $0.50/pound for collected material.

Other services available:

▪ Gift shop.
▪ Shuttle service for float trips.
▪ Store: sells groceries, ice, beer, gasoline, tire service, etc.
▪ Hallie's Hall of Fame: museum honoring west Texas legend Hallie Crawford Stillwell, who helped settle the Big Bend country of west Texas.
▪ Restrooms.
▪ Campground: pull-through RV sites have full hookups; primitive campsites for tent camping; campfires permitted.

Directions: 6 miles off Highway 385 on Farm Road 2627, just north of the main (northern) entrance to Big Bend National Park.

ALPINE / *Native • Difficult*

Hunt for Agates, Precious Opal, and Other Gemstones 𝑇

The following gems or minerals may be found:

▪ Texas red plume agate, moss agate, banded agate, iris agate, quartz, labradorite, pom pom agate, and precious opal

Woodward Ranch
HC 65, Box 40
Alpine, TX 79830
Phone: (915) 364-2271
E-mail: treywoodward@hotmail.com
www.woodwardranch.net

Open: All year, daylight hours, 7 days/week. The Ranch is closed for rockhounding during deer season: Thanksgiving until December 16. The rock shop remains open during this time.

Info: Staff will tell you where to hunt and will sort your "treasure" after you return. Even though the ranch is at an elevation of 5,000 feet, and is usually cool, this is desert, so bring hats, long-sleeved shirts, sunscreen, and lots of water. Screwdrivers can be used to dig with.

Admission: $2.00/person (children under

6 free) plus $2.00/pound, labradorite $1.00/gram. Guide service available for a fee with reservations. Precious opal digging must be escorted.

Other services available:

- Lapidary shop: selection of rocks and minerals, on-site lapidary service, campground-related items, i.e. bottled water, and firewood.
- Mail orders available.
- Field trips to Needle Park for parties of three or more with reservations.
- Restrooms.
- Shower.
- Gift shops.
- New: Ranch heritage and fireplace tour; $2.00/person, children under 6 free.

Campground: RV sites have full hookups, showers, and restrooms. Rates: $20.00/night for two people, more people are charged $2.00/night.

Primitive campground is 2 miles from headquarters, on full-time running stream in oak tree woods. Excellent for hiking and bicycling. Swimming permitted in stream, dogs permitted. Rates: $20.00/night; $10.00/day per car for picknicking. Cabin available in primitive camping area, sleeps 10, full kitchen and bath. One–5 people $100.00/night, 6–10 people $150.00/night.

Directions: Located 16 miles south of Alpine on Hwy. 118 South in the foothills of the Davis Mountains. Turn right at the sign and go 2 miles down an all-weather county road until you see the rock buildings.

MASON / *Native • Difficult*

Hunt for Topaz *T*

The following gems or minerals may be found:

- **Topaz, amber (rarely)**

Seaquist Ranch
Seaquist, Inc.
400 Broad Street
Mason, TX 76856
Phone: (325) 347-5413
E-mail: mseaquist@yahoo.com

Open: All year, but spring is best; summer is hot. Daylight hours, 7 days/week.
Info: This is very rugged terrain. Only picks, shovels, and screening are allowed; no machinery or pumps. Topaz hunters must register in the book in the blockhouse. All topaz hunters are limited to a 3-day hunt.
Admission: Adults $15.00/day/person, children (7–11) ½ price, under 5 no charge.

Pick up the key up from the NuWay store, just off Mason Square on Highway 29.

Campground: Primitive camping $5.00/night, electrical hookup $15.00/night.

THREE RIVERS / *Native • Difficult*

Hunt for Agate and Petrified Wood *T*

The following gems or minerals may be found:

- **Agate, petrified wood**

House Ranch
218 Country Wood
San Antonio, TX 78216
Phone: (210) 490-2433

Open: All year except deer hunting season (November–December), daylight hours, 7 days/week.

Admission: $10.00/day per person, maximum $25.00/day per vehicle (4 or 5 people).

Info: Call ahead of time, or write, and then call near the time you wish to visit (owners are not always home). Get the key and directions to the ranch from the Houses. Ranch is about 9 miles from town.

Directions: The Houses live in San Antonio. See mailing address.

SECTION 2: Museums and Mine Tours

ALPINE

Museum 🏛

Last Frontier Museum and
Antelope Lodge
Teri Smith
2310 W. Highway 90
Alpine, TX 79830
Phone: (432) 837-2451;
(800) 880-8106

Open: Call for hours.

Info: Presents the rocks to be found in the west Texas area. Teri also has a beginning rock hunting class once a month, and sometimes leads groups onto nearby ranches.

Rates: Free.

Other services available: Lodging, gift shop.

Directions: Call for directions.

AUSTIN

Museum 🏛

Texas Memorial Museum of Science
and History
The University of Texas at Austin
2400 Trinity Street
Austin, TX 78705
Phone: (512) 471-1604
www.utexas.edu/tmm/

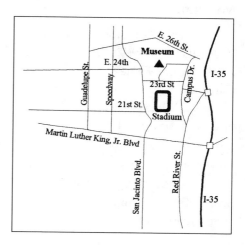

Open: All year, Monday–Friday 9:00 A.M.–5:00 P.M., Saturday 10:00 A.M.– 5:00 P.M., Sunday 1:00–5:00 P.M., closed major holidays. Groups must make advance reservations.

Info: Sparkling displays of gems, minerals, and rocks in the Hall of Geology. Included are mineral specimens from the Barron Collection, a display of Mexican agate, and selected meteorites and tektites.

Admission: Free, contributions encouraged and appreciated.

Other services available: Gift shop.

Directions: Located on the University of Texas Campus at 2400 Trinity Street, approximately 2 blocks south of Memorial Stadium and 3 blocks west of the Lyndon Baines Johnson Library. Free parking can be found at the LBJ Library, or fee parking on weekdays at the University of Texas parking garage north of the Museum.

A.M.–6:00 P.M., Sunday 1:00–6:00 P.M. Group rates available.

Info: The museum's gem and mineral collection contains many rocks and minerals found in the Texas Panhandle. It also contains a very fine group of meteorites and replicas of show-quality gems. The collection is primarily a study tool for researchers in the area and for students at West Texas A&M University; consequently, many specimens are not on display. Exhibit specimens are mostly large, colored crystals such as calcite, selenite, and amethyst.

Admission: Adults $7.00, seniors 65+ $6.00, children 13+ $4.00, children 4–12 $3.00, children under 4 free.

Directions: Located on the West Texas A&M University Campus at 2401 Fourth Avenue, 15 minutes south of Amarillo on I-27.

CANYON

Museum

Panhandle Plains Historical Museum
WTAMU Box 60967
2401 Fourth Avenue
Canyon, TX 79016
Phone: (806) 651-2244
Fax: (806) 651-2250
www.panhandleplains.org

Open: All year, closed major holidays. September–May, Monday–Saturday 9:00 A.M.– 5:00 P.M., Sunday 1:00–6:00 P.M. June–August, Monday–Saturday 9:00

FORT STOCKTON

Museum

Annie Riggs Memorial Museum
301 S. Main Street
Fort Stockton, TX 79735
Phone: (432) 336-2167
Fax: (915) 336-7529

Open: October 1–March 14, Monday–Saturday 9:00 A.M.–6:00 P.M., Sunday 1:00 P.M.–6:00 P.M.; March 15–September 30, Monday–Saturday 9:00 A.M. –8:00 P.M., Sunday 1:00 P.M.–6:00 P.M. Extended hours in the summer.

Info: The museum has exhibits of rocks and minerals from Pecos county and the Big Bend area.

Admission: Call for fees.

Directions: On the corner of South Main and Callaghan Streets in downtown Fort Stockton.

FRITCH

Mine Tour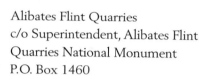

Alibates Flint Quarries
c/o Superintendent, Alibates Flint Quarries National Monument
P.O. Box 1460
419 E. Broadway
Fritch, TX 79036
Phone: (806) 857-3151
Fax: (806) 857-2319
www.nps.gov

Open: Memorial Day–Labor Day, seven days/week. Guided tours by reservation only.

Info: For 12,000 years, people quarried Alibates flint for toolmaking. Indians of the Ice Age Clovis culture used Alibates flint for spear points to hunt mammoths before the Great Lakes were formed. Flint was gathered and used by nomadic people for most of the quarry's history. Prehistoric people needed good material for tools and weapons, and Alibates flint was some of the finest. Between 1150 and 1500, Indians engaged primarily in farming lived around the quarries. They quarried the flint for tools and as trade goods; Alibates flint items have been found throughout the Great Plains and the Southwest.

The tour involves a leisurely walk up a moderately steep trail that is covered with loose gravel in places. Comfortable, sturdy walking shoes are recommended. Alibates flint comes from a 10-square-mile area around Lake Meredith. The quarries consist of a large number of small pits scattered along the edge of the bluffs above the Canadian River.

Flint collecting is prohibited in the National Park. The quarries may be toured only with a guide from the Park Service. Bring your own water. Heat may cause some discomfort during the summer months. During the winter, low temperatures require the use of protective clothing. Though rattlesnakes are found in the area, they are not commonly seen along the trail, and they seldom give any trouble unless disturbed.

Note: No visitor's center or self-guided tours.

The U.S. Army opened the door to settlers in this area in 1874. One of the pioneers, a man named Allie Bates, worked near the flint quarries on a cottonwood-shrouded creek that was later named for him.

Admission: Free.

Directions: Texas Route 136 goes from Amarillo to the Park Headquarters. Alibates Road to the quarries goes off on the left about 7½ miles before the Park Headquarters.

For information on other Native American Stone Quarries, see listings in Newark, DE: jasper quarries (Vol. 4); Calumet and Copper Harbor, MI: copper (Vol. 4); Pipestone, MN: pipestone quarries (Vol.1); and Hopewell and Brownsville, OH: flint quarries (Vol. 4).

HOUSTON

Museum

Houston Museum of Natural Science
1 Houston Circle Drive
Houston, TX 77030
Phone: (713) 639-4629
www.hmns.org

Open: 9:00 A.M.–5:00 P.M., Monday–Saturday; Sunday, 11:00 A.M.–5:00 P.M.
Info: Cullen Hall houses more than 750 gem and mineral specimens, while Eby Hall of Mineral Science presents the history and science of mineralogy.

Admission: Adults $8.00, seniors and children $4.00. Group discounts available.
Other services: Gift shop.
Directions: Call for specific directions.

MARBLE FALLS

Mine View: Granite Mountain

Marble Falls/Lake LBJ Chamber of Commerce
801 Highway 281
Marble Falls, TX 78654
Phone: (830) 693-4449; (800) 759-8178
Fax: (830) 693-7594
www.marblefalls.org

Open: All year. Visitor's Center open Monday–Friday, 8:00 A.M.–5:00 P.M.
Info: Granite Mountain is an 866-foot dome of solid pink granite, covering 180 acres at the western outskirts of the city of Marble Falls. It is a part of the mineral-rich geological environment called the Llano uplift.

Granite

Granite is a stone that is composed of quartz, feldspar, and usually mica. Properly installed, it should last forever. A highly valued quality of granite is that it will accept a high polish. Not only is this mirror finish exceptionally beautiful, but it is especially suitable for resisting extreme conditions.

Granite Mountain was purchased by the Spring Granite Co., of Cold Springs, MN, in 1951, and has operated under the name Texas Granite Corporation since that time. The Cold Springs Granite Co. is said to be the world's largest fabricator of granite products, including interior and exterior structural granite, landscape and industrial granite, and memorials.

Granite from Granite Mountain was used in the construction of many well-known buildings, including the Georgia Pacific Building and the Coca-Cola Building, both in Atlanta, GA; the Wyndham Hotel in Dallas, TX; the Inter-North Building in Omaha, NE; Sohio World Headquarters in Cleveland, OH; and the Crocker building in San Francisco, CA. It was also used for the famed seawall in Galveston, TX, and virtually every jetty on the Texas gulf coast. Although quarrying has continued for almost 100 years, the size of this huge mass has changed very little. There are centuries worth of granite left in this quarry, which is the largest of its kind in the U.S.

Granite Mountain is owned and mined by the Texas Granite Corp., and no tours are offered to the public. However, there is an overlook on Highway 143 from which you can see the mountain and the mining operations taking place. **Admission:** Free.

MCKINNEY

Museum 🏛

The Heard Natural Science Museum & Wildlife Sanctuary
One Nature Place
McKinney, TX 75069-8840
Phone: (972) 562-5566
Fax: (972) 548-9119
E-mail: info@heardmuseum.org
www.heardmuseum.org

Open: All year, Tuesday–Saturday 9:00 A.M.–5:00 P.M., Sunday 1:00–5:00 P.M., closed Thanksgiving, Christmas, and New Year's Day.

Info: The Heard Natural Science Museum & Wildlife Sanctuary brings nature and people together to discover, enjoy, experience, preserve and restore our priceless environment. The 289 acre site enchants visitors of all ages with nature trails, a variety of natural science exhibits including a rock and mineral hall, education programs, and more.

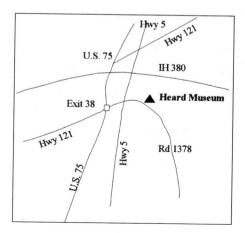

The Museum and Sanctuary owes its existence to the foresight of Miss Bess Heard, a McKinney, Texas, resident and adventurer. On October 1, 1967, Miss Bess opened the Heard Natural Science Museum and started it on its way to its current acreage.

The exhibit halls are currently undergoing renovation, updating the collections Miss Bess established during her long lifetime, and presenting Native Texas minerals, plants, and animals. Among the exhibits is a "stained glass" window made of rock samples.

Admission: Adults $5.00, children 3–12 and seniors $3.00.

Directions: From Dallas, take U.S. 75 North to Exit 38A and follow the signs.

ODESSA

Geologic Landmark 🏛

Odessa Meteor Crater
c/o Thomas E. Rodman
620 N. Grant Avenue, Suite 1204
P.O. Box 3626
Odessa, TX 79760
Phone: (432) 332-1666

Info: The Odessa Meteor Crater is the second largest crater recognized in the U.S. (The largest is the Arizona Crater—see listing under Meteor Crater Enterprises, Inc., Flagstaff, AZ.) The Odessa Crater and four smaller craters were formed in prehistoric times when a shower of nickel-iron meteorites collided with the earth. It is estimated that this event occurred some 50,000 years ago. The Odessa Crater is approximately 500 feet across and was originally 100 feet deep. Wind and rain have gradually filled it in over the centuries until it is only about 15 feet deep today.

A museum at the crater features meteor fragments recovered from the Odessa Meteor Crater. The display also includes samples from other meteorites and information relating to extraterrestrial specimens.

Admission: Free.

Directions: Take West Interstate 20 from Odessa for 5 miles to exit 108/80, then go 2 miles south on Meteor Crater Road. Pick up a brochure at the Chamber of Commerce at 700 N. Grant Street.

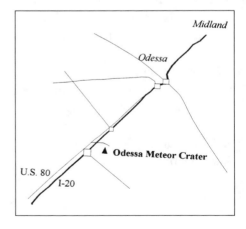

SECTION 3: Special Events and Tourist Information

ANNUAL EVENT

Big Bend Gem and Mineral Show ☛

Held in mid-April of each year.

For more information:
Alpine Chamber of Commerce
106 N. 3rd Street
Alpine, TX 79830
Phone: (432) 837-2326; (800) 561-3735
www.alpinetexas.com

TOURIST INFORMATION

State Tourist Agency ☛

Texas Economic Development Tourism Division
P.O. Box 12728
Austin, TX 78711
Phone: (800) 8888-TEX
www.traveltex.com

UTAH

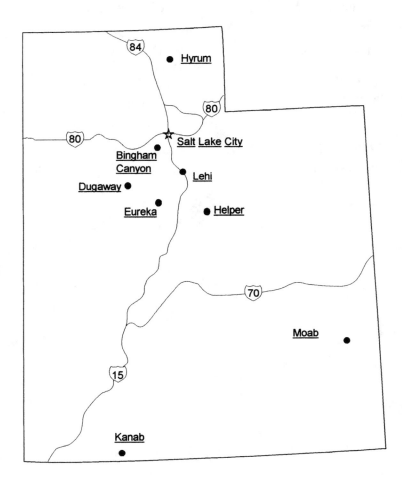

State Gemstone: Topaz
State Mineral: Copper
State Stone/Rock: Coal

DUGAWAY MOUNTAINS /

Native • Moderate

Dig for Geodes 𝑇

The following gems or minerals may be found:

• Geodes

Dugaway Geode Beds
BLM
House Range/Warm Springs Field Office
Phone: (435) 743-3100

Open: All year.

Info: The Dugaway Geode Beds are near the Bonneville Salt Flats. The digging location is marked with signs; look for signs of previous digging. Bring your own equipment: a shovel, pick, safety glasses, and rock hammer. Also, this is a very remote area, be sure you have liquids for drinking, and any other items you may need with you. Be careful of deep holes in soft soils!

Rates: Free.

Directions: Take State Highway 36 south for 40½ miles from I-80. Turn right (west) onto Pony Express Road, and drive 50.1 miles to the Dugaway Geode Bed sign. Turn right (north) and drive up the dirt road and park where you see signs of recent digging.

KANAB

Dig for Septarian Nodules 𝑇

The following gems or minerals may be found:

• Septarian nodules

Joe's Rock Shop
Box 116
Orderville, UT 84758
Phone: (435) 648-2737
E-mail: joesrock@color-country.net

Open: All year by reservation.

Info: Septarian nodules are geodes with a thin wall of calcite separating the clay exterior from the calcite center. Joe's Rock Shop has claims for septarian nodules mining sites, where they allow rockhounds to dig for nodules. Bring your own equipment: a shovel, pick, safety glasses, and rock hammer.

Rates: No charge for digging, but contact the shop owners for permission and information.

Other services available: Rock shop, cutting, and polishing of nodules.

Directions: Directions will be given when arranging for access to the site.

SECTION 2: Museums and Mine Tours

BINGHAM CANYON

Mine Overlook & Visitors Center 🏛

Bingham Canyon Mine Visitors Center
Kennecott Corporation
P.O. Box 351
Bingham Canyon, UT 84044-0351
Phone: (801) 252-3234
Fax: (801) 569-7434

Open: April–October, 8:00 A.M.–8:00 P.M., 7 days/week.

Info: Bingham Canyon Mine is considered the birthplace of open-pit copper mining. An overlook allows visitors to view mining operations in a mine that is more than ¾ mile deep and 2½ miles across. The visitors center shows how copper is produced. It is within the open pit, which is reported to be so large that, other than the Great Wall of China, it is the only other man-made object that can be seen from space.

Admission: Passenger cars $5.00, tour buses $50.00, school buses free. All admission fees are donated to local charities and nonprofit organizations.

Directions: Take the 7200 south exit off I-15 in Salt Lake City, then take State Highway 48 (Bingham Highway) to State Highway 111 to the visitors center. From State Highway 201, take the 8400 west exit, and drive south on State Highway 111 to the visitors center.

EUREKA

Museum 🏛

Tintec Mining Museum
241 W. Main Street
Eureka, UT 84628
Phone: (435) 433-6842; (435) 433-6869

Open: By appointment.

Info: Mineral display collected from mines, model of a mine, and mining tools. It is located in the former Eureka City Hall (1899) and railroad depot.

Admission: Free, donations accepted.

Directions: Eureka is located on U.S. 6, 20 miles west of its junction with I-15, exit 244.

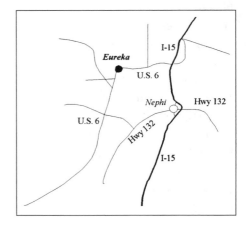

HELPER

Museum 🏛

Western Mining & Railroad Museum
296 S. Main
Helper, UT 84526
Phone: (435) 472-3009
www.wmrrm.org

Open: May 1–September 30, Monday–Saturday, 10:00 A.M.–6:00 P.M. October 1–April 30, Tuesday–Saturday, 11:00 A.M.–4:00 P.M.

Info: Outdoor displays show mining equipment used in mines from the early 1900s up to today. Mining artifacts are displayed, and a simulated 1900 coal mine can be toured. Helper is located in an active coal mining area on the main line of the former Denver and Rio Grande Railroad going to Denver.

Admission: Free; donations accepted.

Other attractions: Historic district, river walk.

Directions: Take U.S. 6 or State Highway 10 north from I-70. Helper is on Route 6 at its intersection with U.S. 191.

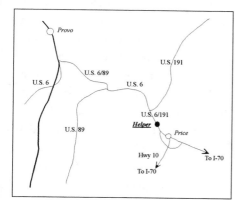

HYRUM

Museum 🏛

Hyrum City Museum
83 W. Main
Hyrum, UT 84319
Phone: (435) 245-6033

Open: Tuesday, Thursday, Saturday, 3:00–5:00 P.M.

Info: Black light display of minerals.

Admission: Free.

Directions: From I-15/84 at Brigham City, take U.S. 89/91 north to State Highway 101. Drive east on State Highway 101 to Hyrum.

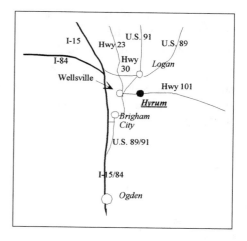

LEHI

Museum 🏛

John Hutchings Museum of Natural History
55 N. Center Street
Lehi, UT 84043

Phone: (801) 768-7180
www.utahvalley.org
www.hutchingsmuseum.org

Open: All year, closed holidays. Tuesday–Saturday 11:00 A.M.–5:00 P.M. Extended hours in the summer. The first Monday of each month, 6:00 P.M.–8:00 P.M., free admission. Closed holidays.

Info: The museum houses one of the finest and most complete private collections of minerals in the country. The displays are linked to the various mining regions and districts and include an exceptional collection from the Bingham mines, including copper, gold, silver, lead, and molybdenum. Also included are rare specimens of varacite, vivianite, US-alite, selenite with water inclusions, and crystal aluminum. The museum has a display of uncut gems, including beryl, sapphire, opal, garnet, topaz, turquoise, Herkimer "diamonds," and kunzite, and also displays cut gemstones.

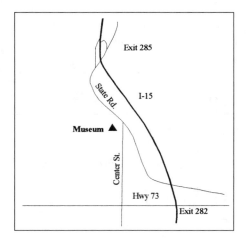

Admission: Adults $2.50, seniors $2.00, children (12 and under) $1.50.

Other services available: Gift shop.

Directions: Take exit 285 off I-15, and travel south on State Road to Center Street. The museum is at the intersection of State Road and Center Street.

SALT LAKE CITY

Museum

Utah Museum of Natural History
University of Utah
1390 E. President's Circle
Salt Lake City, UT 84112
Phone: (801) 581-6927
www.umnh.utah.edu

Open: All year; closed holidays. Monday–Saturday 9:30 A.M.–5:30 P.M. Sunday noon–5:00 P.M.

Info: Mineral Hall in the Utah Museum of Natural History contains cases depicting the structure of minerals and their classifications. There is a large case of fluorescent minerals. A mural shows how minerals are formed. View a replica of a coal mine, complete with sound effects. Mining exhibits include principal metallic and nonmetallic ores found in Utah; Utah's mineral deposits, how and when they were formed; two different methods of mining copper in the Oquirrh mountains; and minerals used for energy. Students can test various uranium ores with a Geiger counter. Minerals used as gemstones, some of which are carved, are also on display.

Admission: Adults $6.00, children (3–12) and seniors $3.50, under 3 free.
Directions: The museum is on the University Campus at the intersection of University Street (1340 East) and President's Circle (215 South).

SECTION 3: Special Events and Tourist Information

MOAB

Place of Interest

Lin Ottinger
Moab Rock Shop
600 N. Main Street
Moab, UT 84532
Phone: (435) 259-7312

Open: 9:00 A.M.–6:00 P.M., 7 days a week.
Info: Map available which shows geological information of the Colorado Plateau, and has information and photographs to show formations good for collecting.

Other services available: Gift shop/museum.

TOURIST INFORMATION

State Tourist Agency

Utah Travel Council
Council Hall/Capital Hill
Salt Lake City, UT 84114
Phone: (801) 538-1030; (800) 200-1160; (800) 882-4386
Fax: (801) 538-1399
www.utah.com

Index by State

ALABAMA

Fee Dig Mines and Guide Services
None

Museums and Mine Tours
Anniston   Anniston Museum of Natural History—gemstones, meteorite, artificial indoor cave

Dora   Alabama Mining Museum—Focus on coal mining

Tuscaloosa   Alabama Museum of Natural History—minerals, meteorite

ALASKA

Fee Dig Mines and Guide Services
Anchorage   Alaska DNR—Pan for gold
Chugach National Forest—Pan for gold

Fairbanks   El Dorado Gold Mine—gold panning
Faith Creek Camp—Pan, sluice, dredge for gold
Gold Dredge No. 8—gold panning
Chena Hot Springs Resort—gold panning

Girdwood   Crow Creek Mine—Pan for gold

McGrath   Moore Creek Mining, LLC—Prospect or dredge for gold

Nome   Nome Beaches—Pan for gold

Talkeetna   Clark/Wiltz Mining—Prospect for gold

Wrangell   St. Elias National Park and Preserve—Pan for gold, hunt for minerals

Museums and Mine Tours
Chicken   The Chicken Gold Camp & Outpost—Gold dredge tour

Fairbanks   El Dorado Gold Mine—working gold mine tour
Gold Dredge No. 8—gold dredge tour
University of Alaska Museum—minerals and gems from Alaska, Arctic Canada, and the Pacific Rim; includes gold and meteorites

Juneau	Juneau–Douglas City Museum—History of gold mining
	Alaska Gastineau Mill and Gold Mine—Mine tour
Nome	The Carrie N. McLain Memorial Museum—History of gold mining
Wasilla	Independence Mine State Historical Park—Mine tour

ARIZONA

Fee Dig Mines and Guide Services

Apache Jct.	Apache Trails Tours—Gold panning
Glendale	William Gardner—Guide service
Goldfield	Goldfield Ghost Town, Scenic Railroad, and Mine Tours—Gold panning
Prescott	Lynx Creek Mineral Withdrawal Area, Prescott National Forest—Pan for gold
Safford	Black Hills Rockhound Area—Dig for fire agates
	Round Hill Rockhound Area—Search for fire agates, chalcedony, small geodes.
Tempe	Fat Jack Mine—Collect amethyst, quartz, garnet, tourmaline, limonite
Wickenburg	Robson's Mining World—Pan for gold

Museums and Mine Tours

Apache Jct.	Superstition Mountain Museum—Geology, minerals, and mining
Bisbee	Queen Mine Tour—Tour a copper mine
Flagstaff	Meteor Crater Enterprises, Inc.—View a meteor crater, museum of astrogeology
	Museum of Northern Arizona—History of Colorado Plateau, geologic models, mineral specimens
Goldfield	Goldfield Ghost Town, Scenic Railroad, and Mine Tours—Gold mine tour, museum, ghost town
Morenci	Phelps Dodge Morenci Copper Mine—Tour an open-pit mine
Phoenix	Arizona Mining and Mineral Museum—3,000 minerals on exhibit, minerals from AZ copper mines, piece of meteor crater meteorite, rocks from original moon landing, spheres, fluorescent mineral display
Sahuarita	ASARCO Mineral Discovery Center—Geology, mining, minerals, and tour of open-pit mine
Sun City	The Mineral Museum—3,000 rocks and minerals from the U.S. and the world, with emphasis on minerals from AZ; Over 150 fluorescent rocks and minerals, most from Franklin and Sterling Hill, NJ
Tempe	Robert S. Dietz Museum of Geology—Mineral displays, seismograph

Tucson	Arizona-Sonora Desert Museum—Mineral collection from Sonoran desert region
	Mineral Museum, University of Arizona—2,100 of 15,000 minerals on display; AZ minerals, meteorites, fluorescents, borate minerals
Wickenburg	Robson's Mining World—Tour old gold mining village
	Vulture Gold Mine—Mine tour

Annual Events

Quartzsite	Gem & Mineral Shows—Mid-January–mid-February
Scottsdale	Minerals of Arizona—Symposium 1 day in March
Tucson	Gem & Mineral Shows—First 2 weeks in February

ARKANSAS

Fee Dig Mines and Guide Services

Hot Springs	Coleman's Crystal Mines—Dig for quartz crystals
Jessieville	Jim Coleman Crystal Mines—Dig for quartz crystals
	Ouachita National Forest, Crystal Mt. Quartz Collecting Site—Collect quartz crystals
Mt. Ida	Fiddler's Ridge Rock Shop and Crystal Mines—Dig for quartz crystals
	Leatherhead Quartz Mining—Dig for quartz crystals
	Ouachita National Forest, Crystal Vista Quartz Collecting Site—Collect quartz crystals
	Sonny Stanley's Crystal Mine—Dig for quartz crystals
	Starfire Mine—Dig for quartz crystals
	Sweet Surrender Crystal Mine—Dig for quartz crystals
	Wegner's Crystal Mine—Dig for quartz crystals
Murfreesboro	Crater of Diamonds State Park—Dig and screen for diamonds, amethyst, agates, barite, calcite, jasper, quartz, other gems
Pencil Bluff	Arrowhead Crystal Mine—Dig for quartz crystals

Museums and Mine Tours

Fayetteville	The University Museum—Quartz and other AR minerals
Little Rock	Geology Learning Center—AR gems, minerals, fossil fuels
State University	A.S.U. Museum—Minerals, many from AR

Annual Events

Mt. Ida	Quartz Crystal Festival and World Championship Dig—Second weekend in October

CALIFORNIA

Fee Dig Mines and Guide Services

Angels Camp Jensen's Pick & Shovel Ranch—Guided prospecting for gold
Coloma Marshall Gold Digging State Historic Park—Gold panning
Columbia Hidden Treasures Gold Mine Tours—Gold panning
Jackson Kennedy Gold Mine—Gold panning
Jamestown Gold Prospecting Adventures, LLC—Gold panning
Lakeport Lake County Visitors Information Center—Search for Lake County "diamonds" or "moon tears"
Mariposa Little Valley Inn—Gold panning
Mesa Grande Himalayan Tourmaline Mine—Look for California tourmaline
Nevada City Malakoff Diggins State Historical Park—Gold panning
Pala Ocean View Gem Mine—Hunt for tourmaline (pink, green, bicolor, and black); smoky crystals; garnets; book mica; smokey crystals; cleavelandite; kunzite; morganite, gossanite; purple lepidolite; muscovite mica; aquamarine
Pine Grove Roaring Camp Mining Co.—Pan for gold, rockhounding
Placerville Gold Bug Mine and Hangtown's Gold Bug Park—Gold panning

Museums and Mine Tours

Allegany Underground Gold Miners Tours and Museum—Tour an active gold mine
Angels Camp Angels Camp Museum—Rocks and minerals; gold stamping mill, mining equipment
Avalon Catalina Island Museum Society Inc.—Exhibits on mining on Catalina Island
Boron Borax Global Visitors Center—Story of borax
Boron Twenty Mule Team Museum—History of area borate mining
Coloma Marshall Gold Discovery State Historic Park—Gold mining exhibit/museum
Columbia Hidden Treasure Gold Mine—Tour of active gold mine
Death Valley Furnace Creek Borax Museum—Rocks and minerals, featuring borax minerals
El Cajon Heritage of the Americas Museum—Rocks, minerals, and meteorites
Fallbrook Fallbrook Gem & Mineral Museum—Gems and minerals
Grass Valley Empire Mine State Historic Park—Hardrock gold mine
Independence Eastern California Museum—Exhibit depicts local mining

Jackson	Amador County Museum—Collection of mineral spheres from CA, UT, NV
	Kennedy Gold Mine Tours—Surface tour of gold mine
Julian	Eagle and High Peak Gold Mine Tours—Hardrock gold mine tour
	Julian Pioneer Museum—Rock and mineral display, gold mining tools and equipment displays
Lucerne	Lake County Museum—Minerals and gems from Lake County, CA
Los Angeles	Natural History Museum of Los Angeles County—52,000 specimens; minerals of CA; native gold, gems, and minerals
Mariposa	California State Mining and Mineral Museum—Gold from CA, gems and minerals from around the world
Needles	Needles Regional Museum—Needles blue agate, Colorado River pebble terrace stones
Nevada City	Malakoff Diggins State Historic Park—History of hydraulic gold mining
Pacific Grove	Pacific Grove Museum of Natural History—Monterey County rocks, fluorescent minerals
Paso Robles	El Paso des Robles Area Pioneer Museum—Display of local minerals
Placerville	Gold Bug Mine and Hangtown's Gold Bug Park—Tour hardrock gold mine
Quincy	Plumas County Museum—Exhibits on silver and copper mining in Plumas County
Rancho Palo Verdes	Point Vicente Interpretive Center—Exhibits on area geology
Redlands	San Bernardino County Museum—45,000 rocks, minerals, and gems
Ridgecrest	Maturango Museum—Small but well-rounded regional gem and mineral collection
Riverside	Jurupa Mountains Cultural Center—Crestmore minerals display, minerals from around the world on display and for sale, family education programs
	Riverside Municipal Museum—Rocks, minerals, gems, and regional geology
	World Museum of Natural History—Fluorescent minerals, meteorites, tektites, over 1,300 mineral spheres
San Diego	San Diego Natural History Museum—26,000 mineral specimens, includes minerals found in San Diego County mines
Santa Barbara	Department of Geological Sciences, U.C.S.B.—Gem and mineral collection, minerals and their tectonic settings
Shoshone	Shoshone Museum—Rock collection reflecting the geology of the area
Sierra City	Kentucky Mine and Museum—Exhibits of local gold and mercury mining

Sonora	Tuolomne County Museum—Gold from local mines
Yermo	Calico Ghost Town—Explore a silver mine
Yreka	Siskiyou County Courthouse—Gold exhibit
Yucca Valley	Hi-Desert Nature Museum—Rock and mineral collection, includes fluorescent minerals

Annual Events
| **Boron** | Rock Bonanza—Weekend before Easter |
| **Coloma** | Marshall Gold Discovery State Historic Park: Gold Rush Days—End of September–beginning of October |

COLORADO

Fee Dig Mines and Guide Services
| **Idaho Springs** | Argo Gold Mill—Pan for gold and gemstones |
| | Phoenix Mine—Pan for gold |

Museums and Mine Tours
Colorado Springs	Western Museum of Mining and Industry—Displays of mining and gold panning
Cripple Creek	Cripple Creek District Museum—Mineral displays
	Molly Kathleen Gold Mine—Gold mine tour
Denver	Denver Museum of Natural History—2,000 specimens, includes gold, topaz, aquamarine, amazonite, and other Colorado minerals
Georgetown	Lebanon Silver Mine—Tour a silver mine
Golden	Geology Museum, Colorado School of Mines—50,000 specimens, minerals from Colorado and from around the world, gemstones and precious metals, cave exhibit
Idaho Springs	Argo Gold Mill—Historic gold mill, mining museum, Double Eagle Gold Mine
	Edgar Experimental Mine—Tour an experimental mine (silver, gold, lead, copper)
	Phoenix Mine—See a working underground hardrock mine (gold, silver)
Leadville	Matchless Mine—Tour a gold mine
	National Mining Hall of Fame and Museum—Story of the American mining industry from coal to gold
Ouray	Ouray County Historical Society—Mineral and mining displays
Salida	Lost Mine Tour—Mangenese mine
Silverton	Mayflower Gold Mill—Tour a gold mill

Old Hundred Gold Mine Tour, Inc.—Gold mine tour

San Juan County Historical Museum—Minerals and gems from the Silverton area

Victor   Mine View—View of Colorado's largest open-pit gold mine

CONNECTICUT

Fee Dig Mines and Guide Services

Roxbury   Green's Farm Garnet Mine—Search for garnets

Museums and Mine Tours

East Granby   Old New-Gate Prison and Copper Mine—Tour an old copper mine

Greenwich   Bruce Museum of Arts and Science—Minerals and rocks

New Haven   Peabody Museum of Natural History—Minerals of New England and the world

DELAWARE

Fee Dig Mines and Guide Services

None

Museums and Mine Tours

Newark   Delaware Academy of Science, Iron Hill Museum—DE minerals, fluorescent minerals

University of Delaware, Mineralogical Museum—5,000 specimens (1,000 on display), crystals, gems, minerals

DISTRICT OF COLUMBIA

Fee Dig Mines and Guide Services

None

Museums and Mine Tours

Smithsonian Institution, National Museum of Natural History—Gems and minerals

FLORIDA

Fee Dig Mines and Guide Services

Ft. Drum   Ft. Drum Crystal Mine (Ruck's Pit)—Collect calcite encrusted fossil shells

Museums and Mine Tours

Deland   Gillespie Museum, Stetson University—Minerals, gemstones, faceting, replica mine, and cave

Mulberry   Mulberry Phosphate Museum—Exhibits on the phosphate industry

Tampa   Ed and Bernadette Marcin Museum, University of Florida—Minerals and gemstones mainly from FL and the western U.S.

GEORGIA

Fee Dig Mines and Guide Services

Cleveland   Gold'n Gem Grubbin—Dig and pan for gold, sapphires, rubies, emeralds, amethyst, topaz

Dahlonega   Consolidated Gold Mine—Gold panning

                    Crisson Gold Mine—Pan gold sands or enriched gemstone ore

Gainesville   Chattahooche-Oconee National Forest—Gold panning

Helen   Gold Mine of Helen, GA—Pan gold sand or enriched gemstone ore

Jackson's Crossroads Dixie Euhedrals—Hunt for amethyst

LaGrange   Hogg Mine—Collect star rose quartz, aquamarine, beryl (rare), black tourmaline

Lincolnton   Graves Mountain—Search for audite, lazulite, pyrophyllite, kyanite, hematite, pyrite, ilmenite, muscovite, fuchsite, barite, sulfur, blue quartz, quartz crystals, microcrystals such as woodhouseite, variscite, strengite, phosphosiderite, cacoxenite, crandallite

Museums and Mine Tours

Atlanta   Fernbank Museum of Natural History—Joachim gem collection containing 400 cut and polished gemstones

                    Fernbank Science Center—Gems, carved opals, meteorites

Cartersville   Weinman Mineral Museum—2,000 specimens, gems and minerals from the state; simulated cave

Dahlonega   Consolidated Gold Mine—Mine tour

                    Dahlonega Gold Museum—Tells the story of the GA Gold Rush

Elberton   Elberton Granite Museum—Granite quarry and products

Helen   Gold Mine of Helen, GA—Mine tour

Macon   Museum of Arts and Science—Display of gems and minerals

Statesboro   Georgia Southern Museum—Collection of rocks and minerals from Georgia's highlands, Piedmont, and coastal regions

Tallapoosa   West Georgia Museum of Tallapoosa—Small collection of local minerals

Annual Events

Jasper   Pickens County Marble Festival—First weekend in October

HAWAII

Fee Dig Mines and Guide Services
None

Museums and Mine Tours

Hawaii Nat'l Park   Thomas A. Jaggar Museum—Museum on vulcanology and seismology; tour of volcano

Hilo   Lyman House Memorial Museum—Rocks, minerals, gems

IDAHO

Fee Dig Mines and Guide Services

Moscow   3-D's Panhandle Gems and Garnet Queen Mine—Guide service, star garnet digging; trips including gold panning.

Spencer   Spencer Opal Mine—Pick through a stockpile for fire opal; pre-arranged digging at mine is a possibility

St. Maries   Emerald Creek Garnet Area—Dig for star garnets

Museums and Mine Tours

Boise   Museum of Mining and Geology—Exhibits on mining and geology

Caldwell   The Glen L. and Ruth M. Evans Gem and Mineral Collection—Agate, jasper, other gemstones, 2,000 cabochons

Orma J. Smith Museum of Natural History—Extensive collection of minerals

Kellogg   Crystal Gold Mine—Mine tour

Staff House Museum—Rocks, minerals, mining equipment

Pocatella   Idaho Museum of Natural History—Displays of specimens from Idaho and the intermountain west

Wallace   Sierra Silver Mine Tour—Mine tour

ILLINOIS

Fee Dig Mines and Guide Services
None

Museums and Mine Tours

Chicago   The Field Museum—92-year-old gem exhibit

Elmhurst	Lizzadro Museum of Lapidary Art—1,300 pieces of cut and polished gems, fluorescent rocks, a birthstone display
Rockford	Burpee Museum of Natural History—Displays of rocks, minerals, and gems
Rock Island	Augustana Fryxell Geology Museum—Rock and mineral musuem
Rosiclare	The American Fluorite Museum—Story of Fluorospur Industry
Shirley	The Funk Gem and Mineral Museum—Gem and mineral collection
Springfield	Illinois State Museum—Gems and minerals, Illinois specimens, birthstones, fluorescents, copper
West Frankfort	The National Coal Museum, Mine 25—Tour a shaft coal mine

INDIANA

Fee Dig Mines and Guide Services

Knightstown	Yogi Bear Jellystone Park Camping Resort—Midwestern gold prospecting

Museums and Mine Tours

Bedford	Land of Limestone Exhibition—History of Indiana Limestone industry
Fort Wayne	Indiana Purdue University at Fort Wayne—Hallway displays of minerals, meteorites, and rocks
Indianapolis	Indiana State Museum—Indiana and regional minerals
Richmond	Joseph Moore Museum of Natural History, Earlham College—Geology exhibit from local Ordovician limestone

IOWA

Fee Dig Mines and Guide Services

None

Museums and Mine Tours

Danville	Geode State Park—Display of geodes
Iowa City	University of Iowa—Displays on state geology
Sioux City	Sioux City Public Museum—Mineralogy exhibit
Waterloo	Grout Museum—Display of rocks and minerals
West Bend	Grotto of the Redemption—Grotto made of precious stones and gems
Winterset	Madison County Historical Society—Rock and mineral collection

KANSAS

Fee Dig Mines and Guide Services
None

Museums and Mine Tours
Ashland Pioneer Krier Museum—Mineral exhibit

Emporium Johnston Geology Museum—Tri-state mining display, geological specimens from Kansas

Galena Galena Mining and Historical Museum—Focus on local lead mining and smelting industry

Greensburg Pallasite Meteorite at the Big Well Museum—Meteorite strike site and 1,000-pound meteorite

McPherson McPherson Museum—Meteorites

KENTUCKY

Fee Dig Mines and Guide Services
Marion Clement Mineral Museum—Fluorite collecting pit

Museums and Mine Tours
Benham Kentucky Coal Mine Museum—Displays on coal mining and formation of coal

Covington Behringen-Crawford Museum—Display of gems and minerals

Lynch Lynch Portal 31 Walking Tour—Walking tour of coal mining facilities

Marion The Clement Mineral Museum—Display of gems and minerals

LOUISIANA

Fee Dig Mines and Guide Services
None

Museums and Mine Tours
New Orleans Louisiana Nature Center—Small collection of gems and minerals

Shreveport Louisiana State Exhibit Museum—Displays on mining and salt domes

MAINE

Fee Dig Mines and Guide Services

Auburn City of Auburn/Feldspar and Greenlaw Quarries—Hunt for apatite, tourmaline, and quartz

Mt. Apatite Farm/Turner Quarry—Hunt for tourmaline, garnet, graphic granite, clevelandite

Bethel Songo Pond Mine—Collect tourmaline and other ME gems and minerals

Poland Poland Mining Camp—Collect tourmaline and other ME gems and minerals

West Paris Perham's of West Paris—Collect tourmaline and other ME gems and minerals

Museums and Mine Tours

Augusta Maine State Museum—Gems and minerals of ME

Caribou Nylander Museum—Minerals of Maine

West Paris Perham's of West Paris—ME gems and minerals; model of a feldspar quarry, model of a gem tourmaline pocket, fluorescents

Annual Events

Augusta Maine Mineral Symposium—3rd weekend in May

MARYLAND

Fee Dig Mines and Guide Services

None

Museums and Mine Tours

Great Falls Maryland Mine Trail—Gold mine trail

MASSACHUSETTS

Fee Dig Mines and Guide Services

None

Museums and Mine Tours

Amherst Pratt Museum of Natural History—10,000 specimens; minerals from New England and around the world, meteorites

Cambridge Harvard University Museum of Cultural and Natural History—Gems, minerals, ores, meteorites

Springfield Springfield Science Museum—Minerals from around the world

MICHIGAN

Fee Dig Mines and Guide Services
Mohawk   Delaware Copper Mine—Search for souvenir copper

Museums and Mine Tours
Ann Arbor   Exhibit Museum of Natural History, University of Michigan—Exhibits of rocks and minerals

Bloomfield Hills Cranbrook Institute of Science—5,000 minerals and crystals from around the world, including hiddenite, gold

Calumet   Mining Museum at Coppertown, U.S.A.—Exhibits on copper mining

Caspian   Iron County Museum and Park—Iron mining complex

Chelsea   Gerald E. Eddy Geology Center—MI rocks, minerals, crystals, and mining

Copper Harbor Fort Wilkins State Park—History of copper mining in the area

Greenland   Old Adventure Copper Mine—Tour underground copper mine

Hancock   The Quincy Mining Company—Tour an underground copper mine

Houghton   The Seaman Mineral Museum—Crystal collection, minerals from the Lake Superior copper district

Hubbell   The Caledonia Copper Mine—Collect copper, silver, epidote, calcite, hematite

Iron Mountain Iron Mountain Iron Mine—Iron mine tour

Lake Linden   Houghton County Historical Museum—Copper mining and refining equipment displays

Mohawk   Delaware Copper Mine—Mine tour

Mount Pleasant Museum of Cultural and Natural History, Central Michigan University—MI rocks and minerals

Negaunee   Michigan Iron Industry Museum—Story of MI iron industry

MINNESOTA

Fee Dig Mines and Guide Services
                 None

Museums and Mine Tours
Calumet   Hill Annex Mine State Park—Tour an open pit iron mine

Chisholm   Ironworld Discovery Center—Iron industry taconite mining tours

                 Minnesota Museum of Mining—Indoor and outdoor exhibits

                 Taconite Mine Tours—Tour of an open-pit iron ore mine

Hibbing   Mahoning Hull-Rust Mine—Observe an open-pit iron mine

Pipestone	Pipestone National Monument—Tour a Native American pipestone quarry
Soudan	Soudan Underground Mine State Park—Tour an underground iron mine
Virginia	Mineview in the Sky—View an open-pit iron ore mine
	Iron Trails Conventions and Visitor's Bureau—Information on mine view sites

MISSISSIPPI

Fee Dig Mines and Guide Services
> None

Museums and Mine Tours

| Starkville | Dunn-Seiler Museum—Mineral and rock collections |

MISSOURI

Fee Dig Mines and Guide Services

| Alexandria | Sheffler Rock Shop—Dig geodes lined with crystals |

Museums and Mine Tours

Golden	Golden Pioneer Museum—Large mineral exhibit
Joplin	Everett J. Richie Tri-State Mineral Museum—Story of area's lead and zinc mining
Kansas City	University of Missouri–Kansas City, Geosciences Museum—Local and regional specimens
Park Hills	Missouri Mines State Historic Site—1,100 minerals, ores, and rocks
Point Lookout	Ralph Foster Museum, College of the Ozarks—Gemstone spheres and fluorescent minerals
Rolla	Mineral Museum, U. of Missouri, Rolla—3,500 minerals, ores, and rocks from 92 countries and 47 states

MONTANA

Fee Dig Mines and Guide Services

Alder	Red Rock Mine—Screen for garnets
Clinton	L◇E Guest Ranch Outfitters—Sapphire mining pack trips
Dillon	Crystal Park Recreational Mineral Collecting Area—Dig for quartz and amethyst crystal
Hamilton	Sapphire Studio—Sapphire mining "parties"

Helena	Spokane Bar Sapphire Mine and Gold Fever Rock Shop—Dig and screen for sapphires and other gems and minerals
Libby	Libby Creek Recreational Gold Panning Area—Pan for gold
Philipsburg	Gem Mountain—Search for sapphires
	Sapphire Gallery—Wash bags of gravel to look for sapphires

Museums and Mine Tours

Butte	Anselmo Mine Yard—Tour of mining facilities and history of area mining
	The Berkeley Pit—Observation point for closed open-pit copper mine
	Butte-Silver Bow Visitors and Transportation Center—Presents information on area geology and its mining, including local gold and silver mining
	Mineral Museum, Montana College of Mineral Science and Technology—Gold, fluorescents, and minerals from Butte and MT
	World Museum of Mining and 1899 Mining Camp—Tour of surface facilities of former silver and zinc mine
Ekalaka	Carter County Museum—Fluorescent mineral display
Lewistown	Central Montana Museum—Rocks, minerals, and yogo sapphires

NEBRASKA

Fee Dig Mines and Guide Services

None

Museums and Mine Tours

Chadron	Eleanor Barbour Cook Museum of Geoscience—Displays of rocks and minerals
Crawford	Trailside Museum—Displays of western Nebraska geology
Hastings	Hastings Museum—Minerals, rocks, fluorescent minerals, and translucent slabs
Lincoln	University of Nebraska State Museum—Displays of rocks, minerals and fluorescent rocks

NEVADA

Fee Dig Mines and Guide Services

Denio	Bonanza Opal Miles, Inc.—Dig fire wood opal
	The Opal Queen Mining Company—Dig crystal, white, and black fire opal

	Rainbow Ridge Opal Mine—Tailings digging for wood opal
	Royal Peacock Opal Mine, Inc.—Dig black and fire opal
Ely	Garnet Fields Rockhound Area—Hunt for garnets
Reno	High Desert Gems and Minerals—Gem mine tours

Museums and Mine Tours

Las Vegas	Nevada State Museum and Historical Society—Natural history of Nevada
Reno	W.M. Keck Earth Science and Mineral Engineering Museum—Collection of minerals and ores
Virginia City	Chollar Mine—Underground mine tour (gold and silver mine)

NEW HAMPSHIRE

Fee Dig Mines and Guide Services

| **Grafton** | Ruggles Mine—Collect up to 150 different minerals |
| **Laconia** | White Mountain National Forest—Collect amethyst, quartz, and mica |

Museums and Mine Tours

| **Dover** | The Woodman Institute—1,300 specimens, including local rocks |

NEW JERSEY

Fee Dig Mines and Guide Services

Cape May	Cape May Welcome Center—Hunt for Cape May "diamonds"
Franklin	Franklin Mineral Museum and Buckwheat Dump—Tailings diggings for fluorescent minerals and franklinite
Ogdenburg	Sterling Hill Mine and Museum—Collect minerals

Museums and Mine Tours

Franklin	Franklin Mineral Museum—Minerals, rocks, local and worldwide fluorescents
Monroe Township	Displayworld's Stone Museum—Minerals, hands-on exhibits
Morristown	Morristown Museum—Specimens from five continents
New Brunswick	Rutgers Geology Museum—Specimens from the zinc deposit at Franklin and the zeolite deposits from Paterson, meteorites
Ogdensburg	Sterling Hill Mine and Museum—Tour old zinc mine
Paterson	The Paterson Museum—Specimens from local basalt flows and basalt flow in the Poona region of India, minerals from NJ and around the world

| Rutherford | Meadowland Museum—Fluorescent minerals, quartz, minerals from NJ |
| Trenton | New Jersey State Museum—Minerals and rocks, including fluorescents and magnetite ore |

Annual Events

| Franklin | New Jersey Earth Science Association Gem and Mineral Show and Outdoor Swap & Sell—Late April |

NEW MEXICO

Fee Dig Mines and Guide Services

Bingham	Blanchard Mines—Collect over 84 different kinds of minerals in a former lead mine
Deming	Rockhound State Park—Collect a variety of semiprecious stones
Dixon	Harding Mine—Harding pegmatite has yielded over 50 minerals
Magdalena	Bill's Gems & Minerals—Collect copper and iron minerals at mine dumps

Museums and Mine Tours

Albuquerque	Geology Museum, University of New Mexico—Displays of NM minerals and geology
	Institute of Meteoritics, University of New Mexico—Meteorites
	New Mexico Museum of Natural History and Science—3,000 specimens with a focus on NM and the southwestern U.S.
	The Turquoise Museum—Turquoise museum
Portales	Miles Mineral Museum—Dispays of minerals, gems, and meteorites
Socorro	New Mexico Bureau of Mines and Mineral Resources—10,000 specimens of minerals from NM, the U.S., and the world

Annual Events

| Socorro | New Mexico Mineral Symposium |

NEW YORK

Fee Dig Mines and Guide Services

Herkimer	Herkimer Diamond Mine and KOA Kampground—Dig for Herkimer "Diamonds"
Middleville	Ace of Diamonds Mine and Campground—Prospect for Herkimer "Diamonds," calcite crystals, and dolomite crystals
North River	Barton Mines—Hunt for garnets

| St. Johnsville | Crystal Grove Diamond Mine and Campground—Dig for Herkimer "Diamonds" |

Museums and Mine Tours

Albany	New York State Museum—Minerals from New York
Hicksville	The Hicksville Gregory Museum—9,000 specimens form the major minerals groups; also NJ zeolites, Herkimer "diamonds," fluorescents
New York	American Museum of Natural History—Gems, meteorites; emphasis on exceptional specimens from the U.S.
Pawling	The Gunnison Natural History Museum—Minerals

NORTH CAROLINA

Fee Dig Mines and Guide Services

Almond	Nantahala Gorge Ruby Mine—Sluice for rubies, sapphires, amethyst, topaz, garnet, citrine, smoky quartz
Boone	Foggy Mountain Gem Mine—Screen for topaz, garnet, aquamarine, peridot, ruby, star sapphire, amethyst, citrine, smoky quartz, tourmaline, emerald
Canton	Old Pressley Sapphire Mine—Sluice for sapphires
Cherokee	Smoky Mountain Gold & Ruby Mine—Sluice for gold and gems
Chimney Rock	Chimney Rock Gemstone Mine—Screen for aquamarine, emerald, ruby, peridot, garnet, quartz, agate, hematite, amethyst, sodalite
Franklin	Cowee Mountain Ruby Mine—Sluice for rubies, sapphires, garnets, tourmaline, smoky quartz, amethyst, citrine, moonstone, topaz
	Gold City Gem Mine—Sluice for rubies, sapphires, garnets, emeralds, tourmaline, smoky quartz, amethyst, citrine, moonstone, topaz
	Mason Mountain Rhodolite and Ruby Mine and Cowee Gift Shop—Sluice for rhodolite, rubies, sapphires, garnets, kyanite, crystal quartz, smoky quartz, moonstones
	Masons Ruby and Sapphire Mine—Dig and sluice for sapphires (all colors), pink and red rubies
	Moonstone Gem Mine—Sluice for rhodolite, rubies, sapphires, garnets, other precious stones
	Rocky Face Gem Mine—Sluice for rubies, rhodolite garnets
	Rose Creek Mine, Campground, Trout Pond, and Rock Shop—Sluice for rubies, sapphires, garnets, moonstones, amethysts, smoky quartz, citrine, rose quartz, topaz
	Sheffield Mine—Sluice for rubies, sapphires, enriched material from around the world

Hiddenite	Emerald Hollow Mine, Hiddenite Gems, Inc.—Rutile, sapphires, garnets, monazite, hiddenite, smoky quartz, tourmaline, clear quartz, aquamarine, sillimanite
Highlands	Jackson Hole Gem Mine—Sluice for rubies, sapphires, garnets, tourmaline, smoky quartz, amethyst, citrine, moonstone, topaz
Little Switzerland	Blue Ridge Gemstone Mine & Campground—Sapphire, emeralds, rubies, aquamarine, tourmaline, topaz, garnets, amethysts, lepidolite, citrine, moonstone, kyanite, and rose, clear, rutilated, and smoky quartz
	Emerald Village—Sapphire, emeralds, rubies, aquamarine, tourmaline, topaz, garnets, amethysts, lepidolite, citrine, beryl, moonstone, kyanite, and rose, clear, rutilated, and smoky quartz
Marion	The Lucky Strike—Gems and gold panning
	Carolina Emerald Mine and Vein Mountain Gold Camp—Mine for gold, emerald, aquamarine, moonstone, feldspar crystals, garnets, smoky, rose, blue and clear quartz, and tourmaline
Marshall	Little Pine Garnet Mine—Dig for garnets
Micaville	Rock Mine Tours and Gift Shop—Dig for emeralds, aquamarine, golden beryl, feldspar, pink feldspar, star garnets, biotite, olivine, moonstone, thulite, and black tourmaline
New London	Cotton Patch Gold Mine—Gold panning
	Mountain Creek Gold Mine—Gold panning
Spruce Pine	Gem Mountain Gemstone Mine—Sapphires, crabtree emeralds, rubies, Wiseman aquamarine
	Rio Doce Gem Mine—Sapphires, emeralds, rubies, aquamarine, tourmaline, topaz, garnets, amethysts, lepidolite, citrine, beryl, moonstone, kyanite, and rose, clear, rutilated, and smoky quartz
	Spruce Pine Gem and Gold Mine—Sapphires, emeralds, rubies, aquamarine, tourmaline, topaz, garnets, amethysts, lepidolite, citrine, beryl, moonstone, kyanite, and rose, clear, rutilated, and smoky quartz
Stanfield	Reed Gold Mine Historic Site—Gold panning
Union Mills	Thermal City Gold Mining Company—Gold panning

Museums and Mine Tours

Asheville	Colburn Earth Science Museum—Collection of mineral specimens from NC and the world
Aurora	Aurora Fossil Museum—Geology of phosphate mine
Franklin	Franklin Gem and Mineral Museum—Specimens from NC and around the world
	Ruby City Gems and Minerals—Specimens from NC and around the world

Gastonia	Schiele Museum—North Carolina gems and minerals
Greensboro	Natural Science Center of Greensboro—Specimens from NC and around the world
Hendersonville	Mineral and Lapidary Museum of Hendersonville, Inc.—Minerals and lapidary arts
Linville	Grandfather Mountain Nature Museum—Specimens from NC
Little Switzerland	North Carolina Mining Museum and Mine Tour—Tour a closed feldspar mine
Spruce Pine	Museum of North Carolina Minerals—Specimens primarily from local mines
Stanfield	Reed Gold Mine Historic Site—Gold mine tour

Annual Events

Franklin	Macon County Gemboree—3rd weekend in July
	"Leaf Looker" Gemboree—2nd weekend in October
Spruce Pine	Original NC Mineral and Gem Festival—4 days at the beginning of August

NORTH DAKOTA

Fee Dig Mines and Guide Services
None

Museums and Mine Tours

Dickinson	Dakota Dinosaur Museum—Rocks and minerals, including borax from CA, turquoise from AZ, fluorescents, aurora crystals from AR

OHIO

Fee Dig Mines and Guide Services

Hopewell	Hidden Springs Ranch—Dig for flint (groups only)
	Nethers Flint—Dig for flint

Museums and Mine Tours

Cleveland	The Cleveland Museum of Natural History—The Wade Gallery of Gems and Minerals has over 1,500 gems and minerals
Columbus	Orton Geological Museum—Rocks and minerals from OH and the world
Dayton	Boonshoft Museum of Discovery—Minerals and crystals
Glenford	Flint Ridge State Memorial—Ancient flint quarrying

Lima   Allen County Museum—Rock and mineral exhibit

OKLAHOMA

Fee Dig Mines and Guide Services
Jet   Salt Plains National Wildlife Refuge—Digging for selenite crystals
Kenton   Black Mesa Bed & Breakfast—Rockhounding on a working cattle ranch
                Howard Layton Ranch—Rockhounding on a working cattle ranch

Museums and Mine Tours
Coalgate   Coal Country Mining and Historical Museum—Mining museum
Enid   The Mr. and Mrs. Dan Midgley Museum—Rock and mineral collection predominantly from OK and the TX shoreline
Noble   Timberlake Rose Rock Museum—Displays of barite roses
Picher   Picher Mining Museum—Lead and zinc mining
Tulsa   Elsing Museum—Gems and minerals

Annual Events
Cherokee   The Crystal Festival and Selenite Crystal Dig—First Saturday in May
Noble   Annual Rose Rock Festival—First Saturday in May

OREGON

Fee Dig Mines and Guide Services
Federal lands   (Baker City, Jacksonville, Medford, Salem, Unity)—Pan for gold

Klamath Falls   Juniper Ridge Opal Mine—Hunt for fire opal
Madras   Richards Recreational Ranch—Dig for thundereggs, agate
Mitchell   Lucky Strike Geodes—Dig for thundereggs (picture jasper)
Plush   Dust Devil Mining Co.—Dig for sunstones
                High Desert Gems & Minerals—Dig for sunstones
Roseburg   Cow Creek Recreational Area—Pan for gold
Yachats   Beachcombing—Collect agates and jaspers

Museums and Mine Tours
Central Point   Crater Rock Museum—Minerals, thundereggs, fossils, geodes, cut and polished gemstones
Corvallis   Oregon State University Dept. of Geosciences—Mineral displays
Hillsboro   Rice Northwest Museum of Rocks and Minerals—Displays of minerals and crystals

Redmond	Peterson's Rock Garden—Unusual rock specimens, fluorescent display
Sumpter	Sumpter Valley Dredge State Historical Heritage Area—View a gold dredge, tour historic gold mine towns

Annual Events
Cottage Grove	Bohemia Mining Days—Four days in July, gold panning and exposition
Prineville	Rockhounds Pow-Wow—Mid-June

PENNSYLVANIA

Fee Dig Mines and Guide Services
Williamsport	Crystal Point Diamond Mine—Dig for quartz crystals

Museums and Mine Tours
Ashland	Museum of Anthracite Mining—Story of anthracite coal
	Pioneer Tunnel Coal Mine—Tour an anthracite coal mine
Bryn Mawr	Museum, Department of Geology, Bryn Mawr College—Rotating display of 1,500 minerals from collection of 23,500 specimens
Carlisle	Rennie Geology Museum, Dickinson College—Gem and mineral display
Harrisburg	State Museum of Pennsylvania—Geology of everyday products
Lancaster	North Museum of Natural History and Science—Worldwide specimens with a focus on Lancaster County
Media	Delaware County Institute of Science—Minerals from around the world
Patton	Seldom Seen Mine—Tour a bituminous coal mine
Philadelphia	Academy of Natural Science—Exhibit of gems and minerals
	Wagner Free Institute of Science—Rocks and minerals
Pittsburgh	Carnegie Museum of Natural History—Gems and minerals
Scranton	Anthracite Museum Complex—Several anthracite coal–related attractions, including mine tours and museums
Tarentum	Tour-Ed Mine—Bituminous coal mine tour
Waynesburg	Paul R. Stewart Museum, Waynesburg College—Outstanding mineral collection
West Chester	Geology Museum, West Chester University—Specimens from Chester County, fluorescent specimens
Wilkes-Barre	Luzerne County Historical Society—Displays on anthracite coal mining
Windber	Windber Coal Heritage Center—Exhibits present the heritage of coal mining

Pittsburgh   The Carnegie Museum of Natural History Gem & Mineral Show—Weekend before Thanksgiving

University Park Mineral Symposium—Three days in May

RHODE ISLAND

Fee Dig Mines and Guide Services
None

Museums and Mine Tours
Providence   Museum of Natural History and Planetarium—Rocks and minerals

SOUTH CAROLINA

Fee Dig Mines and Guide Services
None

Museums and Mine Tours
Charleston   Charleston Museum—Small display of gems and minerals

Clemson   Bob Campbell Geology Museum—Minerals, meteorites, faceted stones

Columbia   McKissick Museum, University of South Carolina Campus—Exhibits on geology and gemstones

South Carolina State Museum—Small display of rocks and minerals

SOUTH DAKOTA

Fee Dig Mines and Guide Services
Deadwood   Broken Boot Gold Mine—Pan for gold

Hill City   Wade's Gold Mill—Pan for gold

Keystone   Big Thunder Gold Mine—Pan for gold

Lead   Black Hills Mining Museum—Pan for gold

Wall   Buffalo Gap National Grasslands—Hunt for agates

Museums and Mine Tours
Deadwood   Broken Boot Gold Mine—Gold mine tour

Hill City   Wade's Gold Mill—Guided tour and displays of mining equipment

Keystone   Big Thunder Gold Mine—Underground mine tour

Lead   Black Hills Mining Museum—Simulated underground mine tour

Homestead Visitors Center—Gold mining displays

Murdo	National Rockhound and Lapidary Hall of Fame—Gems and minerals
Rapid City	South Dakota School of Mines and Technology—Local minerals
	Journey Museum—Geology of Black Hills

TENNESSEE

Fee Dig Mines and Guide Services

| Ducktown | Burra Burra Mine—Dig for garnets, pyrite, chalcopyrite, pyrrhotite, actinolite |

Museums and Mine Tours

Johnson City	Hands On! Regional Museum—Simulated coal mine
Knoxville	McClung Museum—Geology of Tennessee
Memphis	Memphis Pink Palace Museum—Geology and minerals from famous mid-South localities

TEXAS

Fee Dig Mines and Guide Services

Alpine	Stillwell Ranch—Hunt for agate and jasper
	Woodward Ranch—Hunt for agate, precious opal, and others
	Seaquist Ranch—Hunt for topaz
Three Rivers	House Ranch—Hunt for agate

Museums and Mine Tours

Alpine	Last Frontier Museum and Antelope Lodge—Display of rocks of west Texas
Austin	Texas Memorial Museum—Gems and minerals
Canyon	Panhandle Plains Historical Museum—Gems and minerals from the TX panhandle; meteorites
Fort Stockton	Annie Riggs Memorial Museum—Rocks and minerals of Pecos County and the Big Bend area
Fritch	Alibates Flint Quarries—View ancient flint quarries
Houston	Houston Museum of Natural Science—Displays of gem and mineral specimens
Marble Falls	Granite Mountain—View marble mining operations
McKinney	The Heard Natural Science Museum and Wildlife Sanctuary—Rocks and minerals
Odessa	Odessa Meteor Crater—Meteorite crater

Annual Events
Alpine   Alpine Gem Show—Mid-April

UTAH

Fee Dig Mines and Guide Services
Dugaway
Mountains   Dugaway Geode Beds—Dig for geodes
Kanab   Joe's Rock Shop—Dig for septarian nodules

Museums and Mine Tours
Bingham   Bingham Canyon Mine Visitors Center—Overlook for open-
Canyon   pit-copper mine
Eureka   Tintec Mining Museum—Mineral display and mining artifacts
Helper   Western Mining and Railroad Museum—Mining exhibits, simulated
                  1900 coal mine
Hyrum   Hyrum City Museum—Display of fluorescent minerals
Lehi   John Hutchings Museum of Natural History—Minerals linked to
                  mining districts, display of uncut gems
Salt Lake City Utah Museum of Natural History—Mineral classification; UT ores
                  and minerals, fluorescent minerals

VERMONT

Fee Dig Mines and Guide Services
                  None

Museums and Mine Tours
Barre   Rock of Ages Corporation—Watch granite being quarried
Norwich   Montshire Museum of Science—Fluorescent minerals
Proctor   Vermont Marble Exhibit—Story of marble

VIRGINIA

Fee Dig Mines and Guide Services
Amelia   Morefield Gem Mine—Dig and sluice for garnet, quartz, topaz, and
                  many others
Stuart   Fairy Stone State Park—Hunt for staurolite crystals (fairy stones)
Virginia City Virginia City Gem Mine—Pan for quartz, ruby, sapphire, garnet, gold

Museums and Mine Tours

Blocksburg	Virginia Tech Geosciences Museum—Large display of Virginia minerals
Goldvein	Monroe Park—Tour a mine camp, gold panning demonstrations
Harrisonburg	The James Madison University Mineral Museum—Crystals, gems, fluorescent display, specimens from Amelia
Martinsville	Stone Cross Mountain Museum—A museum of "Fairy Crosses," specimens of staurolite
	Virginia Museum of Natural History—Minerals and mining exhibits
Pocahontas	Pocahontas Exhibition Mine and Museum—Coal mine tour
Richmond	University of Richmond Museum—Displays Virginia minerals and a 2,400-carat blue topaz

WASHINGTON

Fee Dig Mines and Guide Services

Olympia Baker	Snoqualmie National Forest—Pan for gold
Ravensdale	Bob Jackson's Geology Adventures—Field trips: collect quartz, garnets, topaz, and others

Museums and Mine Tours

Castle Rock	Mount St. Helens National Volcanic Monument—Focus on geology
Ellensburg	Kittitas County Historical Museum and Society—Polished rocks
Pullman	Washington State University—Silicified wood, minerals
Seattle	Burke Museum of Natural History and Culture—Rocks, minerals, the geology of Washington, and a walk-through volcano

WEST VIRGINIA

Fee Dig Mines and Guide Services

None

Museums and Mine Tours

Beckley	The Beckley Exhibition Coal Mine—Tour a bituminous coal mine
Charleston	The Avampato Discovery Museum at the Clay Center—Exhibits show the story behind West Virginia's geology
Morgantown	Museum of Geology and Natural History—Geology of West Virginia

WISCONSIN

Fee Dig Mines and Guide Services

None

Museums and Mine Tours

Dodgeville	The Museum of Minerals and Crystals—Local mineral specimens, specimens from around the world
Hurley	Iron County Historical Museum—History of area mining, also, last remaining mine head frame in Wisconsin
Madison	Geology Museum, University of Wisconsin at Madison—Minerals, fluorescent minerals, model of Wisconsin cave
Milwaukee	Milwaukee Public Museum—Displays of geological specimens University of Wisconsin at Milwaukee—Minerals
Platteville	The Mining Museum—Lead and zinc mining in the upper Mississippi Valley
Stevens Point	Museum of Natural History—University of Wisconsin—Stevens Point rock and mineral display

WYOMING

Fee Dig Mines and Guide Services

Shell	Trapper Galloway Ranch—Dig for moss agate

Museums and Mine Tours

Casper	Tate Geological Museum—Rocks and minerals, including WY jade, and fluorescent minerals
Cheyenne	Wyoming State Museum—Minerals of Wyoming, coal "Swamp"
Laramie	Geological Museum, University of Wyoming—Rocks and minerals, fluorescent minerals from WY
Saritoga	Saritoga Museum—Minerals from around the world, local geology
Worland	Washaki Museum—Geology of Big Horn Basin

Annual Events

Casper	Tate Geological Museum Symposium on Wyoming Geology—June

Index by Gems and Minerals

This index lists all the gems and minerals that can be found at fee dig mines in the U.S., and shows the city and state where the mine is located. To use the index, look up the gem or mineral you are interested in, and note the states and cities where they are located. Then go to the state and city to find the name of the mine, and information about the mine.

The following notes provide additional information:

(#) A number in parentheses is the number of mines in that town that have that gem or mineral.

(*) Gem or mineral is found in the state, but the mine may also add material to the ore. Check with the individual mine for confirmation.

(FT) Field trip.

(GS) Guide service (location listed is the location of the guide service, not necessarily the location of the gems or minerals being collected).

(I) Mineral has been identified at the mine site but may be difficult to find.

(M) Museum that allows collection of one specimen as a souvenir.

(MM) Micromount (a very small crystal which, when viewed under a microscope or magnifying glass, is found to be a high-quality crystal).

(O) Available at mine but comes from other mines.

(R) Can be found, but is rare.

(S) Not the main gem or mineral for which the site is known.

(SA) "Salted" or enriched gem or mineral.

(U) Unique to the site.

(Y) Yearly collecting event.

Actinolite Tennessee: Ducktown

Agate Arkansas: Murfreesboro (S); Iowa: Bonaporte; Montana: Helena (S); Nevada: Gerlach; New Mexico: Deming (GS); Oklahoma: Kenton (2); North Carolina: Chimney Rock (SA); Oregon: Yachats; South Dakota: Wall; Texas: Three Rivers; Virginia: Amelia

Banded agate Texas: Alpine
Fire agate Arizona: Safford (2)
Iris agate Texas: Alpine
Ledge agate Oregon: Madras
Moss agate Oregon: Madras, Mitchell; Texas: Alpine (2); Wyoming: Shell
Polka-dot jasp-agate Oregon: Madras
Plume agate Nevada: Reno (GS); Oregon: Madras
Pompom agate Texas: Alpine
Rainbow agate Oregon: Madras
Red plume agate Texas: Alpine

Albite Maine: Albany, Poland (GS), West Paris; New Hampshire: Grafton (I); New Mexico: Dixon

Albite (Cleavelandite Var.) Maine: Poland (GS)

Amazonite Virginia: Amelia

Amber Texas: Mason (R); Washington: Ravensdale (GS)

Amethyst Arizona: Glendale; Arkansas: Murfreesboro (S); Georgia: Cleveland, Helen (SA), Jackson's Crossroads; Maine: Bethel (R), West Paris; Montana: Dillon; Nevada: Reno (GS); New Hampshire: Grafton (I), Laconia; New Mexico: Bingham; North Carolina (*): Almond, Boone (SA), Cherokee, Franklin (5), Little Switzerland, Spruce Pine (3)
Amethyst scepters Arizona: Tempe
Crystal scepters Nevada: Sun Valley (GS)

Amblygonite Maine: West Paris

Amphibolite New Hampshire: Grafton (I)

Apatite Maine: Auburn, Bethel, Poland (GS), West Paris; New Hampshire: Grafton; New Mexico, Dixon
Fluorapatite Maine: Poland (GS)
Hydroxylapatite Maine: Poland (GS)
Purple apatite Maine: West Paris

Aplite New Hampshire: Grafton (I)

Aquamarine California: Pala; Georgia: LaGrange; Maine: Bethel, Poland (GS); New Hampshire: Grafton (I); North Carolina (*): Boone (SA), Chimney Rock (SA), Hiddenite, Little Switzerland (2), Marion, Micaville, Spruce Pine (1) (FT)
Brushy Creek aquamarine North Carolina: Spruce Pine (1) (FT)
Weisman aquamarine North Carolina: Spruce Pine (1) (FT)

Aragonite Arizona: Glendale (GS)

Arsenopyrite Maine: Poland (GS)

Augelite Maine: Poland (GS)

Aurichalcite New Mexico: Bingham, Magdalena

Autenite Maine: Poland (GS); New Hampshire: Grafton (I)

Azurite New Mexico: Magdalena; Utah: Moab (GS)

Barite Arizona: Glendale (GS); Arkansas: Murfreesboro (S); Georgia: Lincolnton; New Mexico: Bingham; Washington: Ravensdale (GS)

Beraumite Maine: Poland (GS)

Bermanite Maine: Poland (GS)

Bertrandite Maine: Poland (GS), West Paris

Bertranite New Hampshire: Grafton (I)

Beryl Georgia: LaGrange; Maine: Poland (GS), West Paris; New Mexico, Dixon; North Carolina (*): Little Switzerland (2), Spruce Pine (2); South Dakota: Custer (GS); Virginia: Amelia (2)

    Aqua beryl New Hampshire: Grafton (I)

    Blue beryl (see also aquamarine) New Hampshire: Grafton (I)

    Golden beryl North Carolina: Micaville (FT); New Hampshire: Grafton (I)

Beryllonite Maine: Poland (GS), West Paris

Biotite New Hampshire: Grafton (I); North Carolina: Micaville (FT)

Borate California: Boron (Y)

Bornite New Hampshire: Grafton (I)

Brazilianite Maine: Poland (GS)

Brochantite New Mexico: Bingham

Calcite Arizona: Glendale (GS); Arkansas: Murfreesboro (S); Florida: Ft. Drum; Michigan: Hubbell; New Hampshire: Grafton; New Mexico: Bingham; New York: Middleville; Virginia: Amelia

Cape May "diamonds" See Quartz

Casserite Maine: Poland (GS)

Cassiterite Maine: West Paris

Cerussite New Mexico: Bingham

Chalcedony Arizona: Safford; Nevada: Reno (GS); New Mexico: Deming

Chalcopyrite Tennessee: Ducktown

Childrenite Maine: Poland (GS)

Chrysoberyl Maine: West Paris; New Hampshire: Grafton (I)

Chrysocolla Arizona: Glendale (GS); New Mexico: Bingham

Citrine Georgia: Helen (SA); North Carolina (SA): Almond, Boone, Cherokee, Franklin (6), Little Switzerland, Spruce Pine (3)

Clarkite New Hampshire: Grafton (I)

Clevelandite California: Pala; Maine: Auburn, West Paris; New Hampshire: Grafton (I); New Mexico: Dixon

Columbite New Hampshire: Grafton (I); Maine: Bethel, Poland (GS), West Paris

Compotite New Hampshire: Grafton (I)

Cookeite Maine: West Paris

Copper minerals Michigan: Hubbell, Mohawk (M); New Mexico: Magdalena

Covellite New Mexico: Bingham

Crandalite Georgia: Lincolnton

Cryolite New Hampshire: Grafton (I)

Cuprite New Mexico: Bingham

Cymatolite New Hampshire: Grafton (I)

Dendrites Nevada: Gerlach; New Hampshire: Grafton (I)

Diadochite Maine: Poland (GS)

Diamond Arkansas: Murfreesboro

Dickinsonite Maine: Poland (GS)

Dolomite crystals New York: Middleville

Earlshannonite Maine: Poland (GS)

Elbaite See listing under Tourmaline

Emerald Georgia: Cleveland, Dahlonega (SA); North Carolina (*): Almond, Boone
(SA), Cherokee, Chimney Rock (SA), Franklin, Hiddenite, Little Switzerland (2),
Marion, Micaville (FT), Spruce Pine
  Crabtree Emerald North Carolina: Spruce Pine

Eosphorite Maine: Poland (GS)

Epidote Michigan: Hubbell

Fairfieldite Maine: Poland (GS)

Fairy stones (See Staurolite crystals)

Feldspar Maine: Auburn; New Hampshire: Grafton (I); North Carolina: Marion,
Micaville (FT); Virginia: Amelia
  Albite feldspar Maine: Bethel

Flint Ohio: Hopewell (2)

Fluoroapatite New Hampshire: Grafton (I)

Fluorescent minerals Arizona: Glendale (GS); New Jersey: Franklin; North Carolina:
Little Switzerland; Washington: Ravensdale (GS)

Fluorite New Mexico: Bingham, Socorro (Y); South Dakota: Custer (GS); Virginia:
Amelia; Washington: Ravensdale (GS)
  Aqua Fluorite Arizona: Glendale (GS)

Franklinite New Jersey: Franklin

Gahnite (spinel) Maine: Poland (GS), West Paris

Gainsite Maine: Poland (GS)

Galena Arizona: Glendale (GS); New Mexico: Bingham

Garnets Arizona: Tempe; California: Pala; Connecticut: Roxbury; Georgia: Dahlonega (SA), Helen (SA); Idaho: St. Maries; Maine: Auburn, Bethel, Poland (GS), West Paris; Montana: Alder, Helena (S); New Hampshire: Grafton (I); New Mexico: Dixon; New York: North River; North Carolina (*): Almond, Boone, Canton, Cherokee, Chimney Rock, Franklin (4), Hiddenite, Highlands, Little Switzerland (2), Marion, Marshall, Spruce Pine (3) (FT); Nevada: Ely; Tennessee: Ducktown; Virginia: Virginia City (SA); Washington: Ravensdale (GS)
  Almandine garnets Maine: Poland (GS); Nevada: Ely
  Pyrope garnets North Carolina: Franklin
  Rhodolite garnets North Carolina: Franklin (5)

Garnets, Star Idaho: Moscow (GS), St. Maries; North Carolina: Micaville (FT)

Geodes Arizona: Safford; Missouri: Alexandria; New Mexico: Deming; Utah: Dugaway Mountains
  Lined with:
  Agate, blue New Mexico: Deming
  Aragonite Missouri: Alexandria
  Barites Missouri: Alexandria
  Chalcedony New Mexico: Deming
  Dolomite Missouri: Alexandria
  Goethite Missouri: Alexandria
  Hematite Missouri: Alexandria
  Kaoline Missouri: Alexandria
  Opal, common New Mexico: Deming
  Quartz New Mexico: Deming
  Selenite needles Missouri: Alexandria
  Sphalerite Missouri: Alexandria

Gold (*) Alaska: Anchorage, Chugach, Copper Center, Fairbanks (3), Girdwood, McGrath, Nome, Talkeetna; Arizona: Apache Junction, Goldfield, Prescott, Wickenburg; California, Angels Camp (GS), Coloma, Columbia, Jackson, Jamestown, Mariposa, Nevada City, Pine Grove, Placerville; Colorado: Idaho Springs (2); Georgia: Cleveland, Dahlonega (2), Gainesville, Helen; Idaho: Moscow (GS); Indiana: Knightstown; Montana: Alder (O), Helena, Libby; North Carolina: Cherokee, Marion, New London (2), Stanfield, Union Mills; Oregon: Baker City, Jacksonville, Medford, Rosebury, Salem, Unity; South Dakota: Deadwood, Keystone, Lead; Virginia: Virginia City (SA); Washington: Olympia

Gossanite California: Pala

Goyazite Maine: Poland (GS)

Graftonite Maine: Poland (GS); New Hampshire: Grafton (I)

Granite, graphic Maine: Auburn

Gummite New Hampshire: Grafton (I)

Hedenburgite New Mexico: Magdalena

Hematite Georgia: Lincolnton; Michigan: Hubbell; Montana: Helena; New Mexico: Magdalena; North Carolina: Chimney Rock (SA)

Hemimorphite New Mexico: Bingham

Herderite, hydroxyl Maine: Bethel, Poland (GS), West Paris

Herkimer "diamonds" See Quartz

Heterosite Maine: Poland (GS)

Hiddenite (spodumene) North Carolina: Hiddenite

Hureaylite Maine: Poland (GS)

Iron minerals New Mexico: Magdalena

Iron ore Michigan: Iron Mountain (M)

Jade California: Pine Grove

Jadite Montana: Helena (S)

Jahnsite Maine: Poland (GS)

Jasper Arkansas: Murfreesboro (S); California: Pine Grove; Montana: Helena (S); Oklahoma: Kenton; Oregon: Madras, Yachats; Texas: Alpine
  Brown jasper New Mexico: Deming
  Chocolate jasper New Mexico: Deming
  Orange jasper New Mexico: Deming
  Picture jasper Oregon: Mitchell
  Pink jasper New Mexico: Deming
  Variegated jasper New Mexico: Deming
  Yellow jasper New Mexico: Deming

Jarosite Georgia: Lincolnton; New Mexico: Bingham

Kaolinite Maine: Poland (GS)

Kasolite New Hampshire: Grafton (I)

Kosnarite Maine: Poland (GS)

Kyanite Georgia: Lincolnton; North Carolina (*): Franklin, Little Switzerland

Labradorite Texas: Alpine

Lake County "diamonds" See Quartz

Landsite Maine: Poland (GS)

Laueite Maine: Poland (GS)

Lazulite Georgia: Lincolnton

Lepidolite Maine: Poland (GS), West Paris; New Mexico: Dixon; North Carolina (*): Little Switzerland
  Lemon Yellow Lepidolite New Hampshire: Grafton (I)
  Purple Lepidolite California: Pala

Lepidomelane New Hampshire: Grafton (I)

Limanite Arizona: Tempe

Linarite New Mexico: Bingham

Lithiophyllite Maine: Poland (GS); New Hampshire: Grafton (I)

Lollingite Maine: Poland (GS)

Ludlamite Maine: Poland (GS)

Magnesium oxide See Psilomellane

Magnesium oxide minerals New Mexico: Deming

Malachite New Mexico: Magdalena; Utah: Moab (GS)

Manganapatite New Hampshire: Grafton (I)

Manganese minerals New Mexico: Deming

Manganese oxide minerals New Mexico: Deming

Marcasite New Hampshire: Grafton (I)

McCrillisite Maine: Poland (GS)

Mica Maine: Poland (GS), West Paris; New Hampshire: Grafton (I), Laconia; North Carolina: Canton; South Dakota: Custer (GS); Virginia: Amelia
    Book mica California: Pala
    Muscovite mica California: Pala

Microcline Maine: Poland (GS)

Microlite New Mexico: Dixon

Mitridatite Maine: Poland (GS)

Molybdenite New Hampshire: Grafton

Montebrasite Maine: Poland (GS)

Montmorillonite Maine: Poland (GS), West Paris; New Hampshire: Grafton (I)

Monzaite Maine: Poland (GS)

Moonstone North Carolina (*): Franklin (4), Highlands, Little Switzerland, Marion, Micaville (FT)

Moraesite Maine: Poland (GS)

Morganite California: Pala

Murdochite New Mexico: Bingham

Muscovite Georgia: Lincolnton; New Hampshire: Grafton (I); New Mexico: Dixon

Olivine North Carolina: Micaville (FT)

Opal
    Black opal Nevada: Orovado
    Black fire opal Nevada: Denio
    Common opal New Mexico: Deming

Crystal Nevada: Denio
Fire opal Nevada: Denio, Orovado, Reno (GS); Oregon: Klamath Falls
Hyalite opal Maine: Bethel
Precious opal Idaho: Spencer; Texas: Alpine
Virgin Valley Nevada: Reno (GS)
White opal Nevada: Denio
Wood opal Nevada: Denio

Orthoclase Maine: Poland (GS)

Perhamite Maine: Poland (GS)

Parsonite New Hampshire: Grafton (I)

Perlite (black to gray) New Mexico: Deming

Peridot Arkansas: Murfreesboro (S); North Carolina (*): Boone (SA), Chimney Rock (SA), Franklin

Petalite Maine: Poland (GS), West Paris

Phenakite Virginia: Amelia

Phosphosiderite Georgia: Lincolnton; Maine: Poland (GS)

Phosphouranylite Maine: Poland (GS)

Phosphyanylite New Hampshire: Grafton (I)

Pitch Stone with seams of red & brown New Mexico: Deming

Plattnerite New Mexico: Bingham

Pollucite Maine: Poland (GS), West Paris

Psilomelane New Hampshire: Grafton (I)

Purpurite Maine: Poland (GS); New Hampshire: Grafton (I)

Pyrite Georgia: Lincolnton; Maine: Bethel, Poland (GS); New Hampshire: Grafton (I); New Mexico: Magdalena; Tennessee: Ducktown; Virginia: Amelia, Virginia City (SA); Washington: Ravensdale (GS)

Pyrophyllite Georgia: Lincolnton

Pyrrhotite New Hampshire: Grafton (I); Tennessee: Ducktown

Quartz Arizona: Glendale (GS), Tempe; Arkansas: Hot Springs, Jessieville (2), Mt. Ida (6) (Y), Murfreesboro (S), Pencil Bluff; California: Pine Grove; Colorado: Lake George; Georgia: Lincolnton; Maine: Poland (GS); Montana: Dillon, Helena (S); New Hampshire: Grafton, Laconia; New Mexico: Bingham, Deming, Dixon, Socorro (Y); North Carolina: Chimney Rock; Pennsylvania: Williamsport; Texas: Alpine; Virginia: Amelia, Virginia City (SA); Washington: Ravensdale (GS)

Blue Georgia: Lincolnton; North Carolina: Marion
Clear North Carolina (*): Franklin, Hiddenite, Little Switzerland, Marion, Spruce Pine
Milky Maine: Bethel
Parallel growth Maine: West Paris

Pseudocubic crystals Maine: West Paris

Rose Georgia: Helen (SA); Maine: Auburn; New Hampshire: Grafton (I); North Carolina (*): Franklin, Little Switzerland, Marion

Rose (gem quality) Maine: West Paris

Rutilated North Carolina (*): Little Switzerland, Spruce Pine

Smoky Georgia: Helen (SA); Maine: Bethel; Nevada: Reno (GS); New Hampshire: Grafton (I); North Carolina (*): Almond, Boone (SA), Cherokee, Franklin (5), Hiddenite, Highlands, Little Switzerland (2), Marion, Spruce Pine (2)

Smoky (gem quality) Maine: West Paris

Stone Rose Georgia: LaGrange

Quartz "diamonds"

Lake Co. "diamonds" (moon tears) California: Lake County

Cape May "diamonds" New Jersey: Cape May

Herkimer "diamonds" New York: Herkimer, Middleville, St. Johnsville

Reddingite Maine: Poland (GS); New Hampshire: Grafton (I)

Rhodochrosite Maine: Poland (GS)

Rhodolite (garnet) North Carolina: Franklin (1)

Rochbridgeite Maine: Poland (GS)

Rose rocks See Barite Rose

Rubies California: Pine Grove; Georgia: Cleveland, Dahlonega (SA); Montana: Helena (R); North Carolina (*): Almond, Boone (SA); Cherokee, Franklin (10), Highlands, Little Switzerland (2), Spruce Pine (3); Virginia: Virginia City (SA)

Rutile Georgia: Lincolnton; Maine: Bethel, Poland (GS); North Carolina: Franklin (1), Hiddenite; Virginia: Amelia

Safflorite New Hampshire: Grafton (I)

Sapphires Georgia: Cleveland, Dahlonega (SA); Montana: Alder (O), Clinton (GS), Gem Mountain, Hamilton, Helena (2), Philipsburg; North Carolina (*): Almond, Canton, Cherokee, Franklin (10), Hiddenite, Highlands, Little Switzerland (2), Spruce Pine; Virginia: Virginia City (SA)

Star Sapphire North Carolina: Boone (SA)

Scheelite Maine: West Paris

Selenite crystals New Mexico: Bingham; Oklahoma: Jet (Y)

Septarian nodules Utah: Kanab

Serpentine Montana: Helena (S)

Siderite Maine: Bethel

Silica minerals New Mexico: Deming

Sillimanite New Hampshire: Grafton (I); North Carolina (*): Franklin (1), Hiddenite

Silver Michigan: Hubbell

Smithsonite Arizona: Glendale (GS); New Mexico: Bingham, Magdalena, Socorro (Y)

Sodalite North Carolina: Chimney Rock (SA)

Spangolite New Mexico: Bingham

Spessartine New Mexico: Dixon

Spodumene Maine: Poland (GS), West Paris; New Mexico: Dixon
   Altered Spodumene Maine: West Paris
   Hiddenite North Carolina: Hiddenite

Staurolite New Hampshire: Grafton (I); Virginia: Stuart

Stewartite Maine: Poland (GS)

Strengite Georgia: Lincolnton

Strunzite Maine: Poland (GS)

Sulfur Georgia: Lincolnton

Sunstones Nevada: Reno (GS); Oregon: Plush

Switzerite Maine: Poland (GS)

Tantalite-Columbite New Mexico: Dixon; Virginia: Amelia

Thulite North Carolina: Micaville (FT)

Thundereggs New Mexico: Deming; Oregon: Madras, Mitchell

Tobernite New Hampshire: Grafton (I)

Topaz Georgia: Cleveland, Helen (SA); Maine: Poland (GS); Montana: Helena (R); New Hampshire: Grafton (I); North Carolina (SA): Almond, Boone, Cherokee, Franklin (5), Little Switzerland (3), Spruce Pine (3); Texas: Mason; Virginia: Amelia
   Phenakite crystals in topaz Colorado
   Pink topaz Washington: Ravensdale (GS)

Torberite Maine: Poland (GS)

Tourmaline Arizona: Tempe; California: Mesa Grande; Maine: Auburn (2), Poland (GS), West Paris; North Carolina (*): Boone (SA) Franklin (6), Hiddenite, Highlands, Little Switzerland (3), Spruce Pine (3) (FT); Virginia: Amelia
   Bi-colored California: Pala
   Black tourmaline California: Pala; Georgia: LaGrange; Maine: Auburn, Bethel, Poland (GS), West Paris; New Hampshire: Grafton (I); North Carolina: Micaville (FT)
   Gem tourmaline Maine: West Paris
   Green tourmaline California: Pala; Maine: West Paris
   Pink tourmaline California: Pala

Triphyllite Maine: Poland (GS), West Paris; New Hampshire: Grafton (I)

Triplite Maine: Poland (GS)

Turquoise Nevada: Reno (GS)

Uralolite Maine: Poland (GS)

Uranite Maine: Poland (GS); New Hampshire: Grafton (I) (Species with gummite—world-famous)

Uranium minerals New Hampshire: Grafton (I)

Uranophane New Hampshire: Grafton (I)

Vandendriesscheite New Hampshire: Grafton (I)

Variscite Georgia: Lincolnton; Nevada: Reno (GS)

Vesuvianite Maine: Poland (GS), West Paris (1)

Vivianite New Hampshire: Grafton (I)

Voelerkenite New Hampshire: Grafton (I)

Wardilite Maine: Poland (GS)

Whitlockite Maine: Poland (GS)

Whitmoreite Maine: Poland (GS)

Willemite Arizona: Glendale (GS)

Wodginite Maine: Poland (GS)

Wulfenite Arizona: Glendale (GS); New Mexico: Bingham

Zircon Maine: Bethel, Poland (GS), West Paris; New Hampshire: Grafton (I); North Carolina: Canton

Annual Events

JANUARY

Quartzite, AZ, Gem and Mineral Shows—Mid-January–mid-February

FEBRUARY

Tucson, AZ, Gem and Mineral Show—First two weeks in February

MARCH

Scottsdale, AZ, Minerals of Arizona Symposium—1 day in March each year, sponsored by the Arizona Mineral & Mining Museum Foundation and the Arizona Department of Mines & Mineral Resources

Boron, CA, Rock Bonanza—Weekend before Easter

APRIL

Alpine, TX, Alpine Gem Show—Mid-April

MAY

Cherokee, OK, The Crystal Festival and Selenite Crystal Dig—First Saturday in May

Augusta, ME, Maine Mineral Symposium—Third weekend in May

Poland, ME, Maine Pegmatite Workshop—End of May

JUNE

Prineville, OR, Rockhounds Pow-Wow—Mid-June

Casper, WY, Tate Geological Museum Symposium on Wyoming Geology

JULY

Franklin, NC, Macon County Gemboree—Third weekend in July

Cottage Grove, OR, Bohemia Mining Days—Four days in July

AUGUST

Spruce Pine, NC, Original North Carolina Mineral and Gem Festival—Four days at the beginning of August

Pittsburgh, PA, Carnegie Museum of Natural History Gem and Mineral Show—Last weekend in August

SEPTEMBER

No information available.

OCTOBER

Coloma, CA, Marshall Gold Discovery State Park Gold Rush Days—End of September–beginning of October

Dahlonega, GA, Gold Rush Days—Third weekend in October

Jasper, GA, Pickens County Marble Festival—First weekend in October

Mt. Ida, AR, Quartz Crystal Festival and World Championship Dig—Second weekend in October

Franklin, NC, "Leaf Looker" Gemboree—Second weekend in October

NOVEMBER

Socorro, NM, New Mexico Mineral Symposium—Two days in November

DECEMBER

No information available.

State Gem and Mineral Symbols

STATE	GEMSTONE	MINERAL	STONE/ROCK
Alabama	Star Blue Quartz (1990)	Hematite (1967)	Marble (1969)
Alaska	Jade (1968)	Gold (1968)	
Arizona	Turquoise (1974)	Fire agate	Petrified Wood
Arkansas	Diamond	Quartz crystal	Bauxite
California	Benitoite	Gold	Serpentine (1965)
Colorado	Aquamarine (1971)	Rhodochrosite	
Connecticut	Garnet (1977)		
Delaware			Sillimanite
Florida	Moonstone		Agatized coral
Georgia	Quartz	Staurolite	
Hawaii	Black Coral		
Idaho	Star Garnet (1967)		
Illinois		Fluorite (1965)	
Indiana			Limestone
Iowa			Geode
Kansas			
Kentucky	Freshwater Pearl	Coal	Kentucky Agate
Louisiana	Agate		Petrified Palm
Maine	Tourmaline (1971)		
Maryland		Patuxent River Stone	
Massachusetts	Rhodonite	Babingtonite	Plymouth Rock, Dighton Rock, Roxbury Conglomerate
Michigan	Isle Royal Greenstone (Chlorostrolite) (1972)		Petosky Stone (1965)
Minnesota	Lake Superior Agate		
Mississippi			Petrified Wood (1976)
Missouri		Galena (1967)	Mozarkite (1967)

STATE	GEMSTONE	MINERAL	STONE/ROCK
Montana	Yogo Sapphire & Agate (1969)		
Nebraska	Blue Agate (1967)		Prairie Agate (1967)
Nevada	Virgin Valley Blackfire Opal (1987) (Precious) Turquoise (1987) (Semiprecious)	Silver (Official Metal)	Sandstone (1987)
New Hampshire	Smoky Quartz	Beryl	Granite
New Jersey			Stockton Sandstone
New Mexico	Turquoise (1967)		
New York	Garnet (1969)		
North Carolina	Emerald (1973)		Granite/Unakite
North Dakota			Teredo Wood
Ohio	Flint (1965)		
Oklahoma			Barite Rose
Oregon	Sunstone (1987)		Thundereggs (1965)
Pennsylvania			Trilobite
Rhode Island		Bowenite	Cumberlandite
South Carolina	Amethyst		Blue Granite
South Dakota	Fairburn Agate (1966)	Rose Quartz (1966) (Mineral/Stone)	
Tennessee	Tennessee River Pearls	Tennessee Limestone and Agate	
Texas	Texas Blue Topaz (1969) Lone Star Cut (1977) (Gemstone Cut)		Petrified Palmwood (1960)
Utah	Topaz	Copper	Coal
Vermont	Grossular Garnet	Talc	Granite, Marble, Slate
Virginia			
Washington	Petrified Wood (1975)		
West Virginia	Mississippian Coral, Lithostrotionella		
Wisconsin	Ruby	Galena (1971)	Wausau Red Granite (1971)
Wyoming	Nephrite Jade (1967)		

Finding Your Own Birthstone

Following is a listing of fee dig sites presented in this four-volume guide where you can find your birthstone! Refer to the individual mine listings for more information on individual mines.

Garnet (January Birthstone) Arizona: Tempe; California: Pala; Connecticut: Roxbury; Georgia: Dahlonega (SA), Helen (SA); Idaho: St. Maries; Maine: Auburn, Bethel, Poland (GS), West Paris; Montana: Alder, Helena (S); Nevada: Reno (GS); New Hampshire: Grafton (I); New Mexico: Dixon; New York: North River; North Carolina (*): Almond, Boone (SA), Cherokee, Chimney Rock (SA), Franklin (5), Hiddenite, Highlands, Little Switzerland (2), Marshall, Spruce Pine (3) (FT); Nevada: Ely; Virginia: Virginia City (SA); Washington: Ravensdale (GS)
Almandine garnets Maine: Poland (GS); Nevada: Ely
Pyrope garnets North Carolina: Franklin
Rhodolite garnets North Carolina: Franklin (5)

Amethyst (February Birthstone) Arizona: Glendale (GS); Arkansas: Murfreesboro(S); Georgia: Cleveland, Helen (SA), Jackson's Crossroads; Maine: Bethel (R), West Paris; Montana: Dillon; Nevada: Reno (GS), Sun Valley (GS) (crystal scepters); New Hampshire: Grafton (I), Laconia; New Mexico: Bingham; North Carolina (*): Almond, Boone (SA), Cherokee, Chimney Rock (SA), Franklin (4), Highlands, Little Switzerland, Spruce Pine (3)
Amethyst scepters Arizona: Tempe

Aquamarine or Bloodstone (March Birthstone):
Aquamarine Georgia: LaGrange; Maine: Bethel, Poland (GS); New Hampshire: Grafton (I); North Carolina (*): Boone (SA), Chimney Rock (SA), Hiddenite, Little Switzerland (5), Marion, Micaville (FT), Spruce Pine (1) (FT)
Brushy Creek Aq. North Carolina: Spruce Pine (FT)
Weisman Aq. North Carolina: Spruce Pine (FT)
Bloodstone No listing

Diamond (April Birthstone) Arkansas: Murfreesboro

Emerald (May Birthstone) Georgia: Cleveland, Dahlonega (SA); North Carolina (*): Boone (SA), Cherokee, Chimney Rock (SA), Franklin, Hiddenite, Little Switzerland (2), Marion, Micaville, Spruce Pine (1)
Crabtree Emerald North Carolina: Spruce Pine

Moonstone or Pearl (June Birthstone):
Moonstone North Carolina (*): Franklin (6), Little Switzerland, Marion, Spruce Pine
Pearl No listing

Ruby (July Birthstone) Georgia: Cleveland, Dahlonega (SA); Montana: Helena (R); North Carolina (*): Boone (SA), Cherokee, Chimney Rock (SA), Franklin (11), Highlands, Little Switzerland (2), Spruce Pine (3); Virginia: Virginia City (SA)

Peridot or Sardonyx (August Birthstone):
Peridot Arkansas: Murfreesboro (S); North Carolina (*): Franklin
Sardonyx No listing

Sapphire (September Birthstone) Georgia: Dahlonega (SA); Montana: Alder (O), Clinton (GS), Gem Mountian, Hamilton, Helena (2), Philipsburg; North Carolina (*): Boone (SA) Canton, Cherokee, Franklin (13), Hiddenite, Highlands, Little Switzerland (2), Spruce Pine; Virginia: Virginia City (SA)

Opal or Tourmaline (October Birthstone):
Opal
    Black opal Nevada: Orovado
    Black fire opal Nevada: Denio
    Common opal New Mexico: Deming
    Crystal opal Nevada: Denio
    Fire opal Nevada: Orovado, Reno (GS); Oregon: Klamath Falls
    Hyalite opal Maine: Bethel
    Precious opal Idaho: Spencer; Texas: Alpine
    Virgin Valley Nevada: Reno (GS)
    White opal Nevada: Denio
    Wood opal Nevada: Denio
Tourmaline Arizona: Tempe; California: Mesa Grande; Maine: Auburn (2), Poland (GS), West Paris; North Carolina (*): Boone (SA), Franklin (6), Hiddenite, Highlands, Little Switzerland (3), Micaville (FT), Spruce Pine (2) (FT); Virginia: Amelia
    Black tourmaline California: Pala; Georgia: LaGrange; Maine: Auburn, Bethel, Poland (GS), West Paris; New Hampshire: Grafton (I)
    Gem tourmaline Maine: West Paris
    Green tourmaline California: Pala; Maine: West Paris
    Pink tourmaline California: Pala

Topaz (November Birthstone) Georgia: Cleveland, Helen (SA); Maine: Poland (GS); Montana: Helena (R); New Hampshire: Grafton (I); North Carolina (SA): Cherokee, Chimney Rock (SA), Franklin (6), Little Switzerland (3), Spruce Pine (3); Texas: Mason (2); Virginia: Amelia
    Pink topaz Washington: Ravensdale (GS)

Turquoise or Lapis Lazuli (December Birthstone):
Turquoise Nevada: Reno (GS)
Lapis Lazuli No listing

The preceding list of birthstones is taken from a list adopted in 1912 by the American National Association of Jewelers ("The Evolution of Birthstones" from *Jewelry & Gems—The Buying Guide* by Antoinette Matlins and A. C. Bonanno; Gemstone Press, 2005).

Finding Your Anniversary Stone

The following is a listing of fee dig sites contained in this four-volume guide where you can find the stone that is associated with a particular anniversary.

First: Gold (Jewelry) Alaska: Anchorage, Chugach, Fairbanks (3), Girdwood, McGrath, Nome, Talkeetna, Wrangell; Arizona: Goldfield, Prescott, Wickenburg; California: Angels Camp (GS), Coloma, Columbia, Jackson, Jamestown, Mariposa, Nevada City, Pine Grove, Placerville; Colorado: Idaho Springs (2); Georgia: Cleveland, Dahlonega (2), Helen; Idaho: Moscow (GS); Indiana: Knightstown; Montana: Alder (O), Helena, Libby; North Carolina: Cherokee, Marion, New London, Stanfield, Union Mills; Oregon: Baker City, Jacksonville, Medford, Rosebury, Salem, Unity; South Dakota: Deadwood, Keystone, Lead; Virginia: Virginia City (SA); Washington: Olympia

Second: Garnet Arizona: Tempe; California: Pala; Connecticut: Roxbury; Georgia: Dahlonega (SA), Helen (SA); Idaho: St. Maries; Maine: Auburn, Bethel, Poland (GS), West Paris; Montana: Alder, Helena (S); New Hampshire: Grafton (I); New Mexico: Dixon; New York: North River; North Carolina (*): Almond, Boone (SA), Cherokee, Chimney Rock (SA), Franklin (5), Hiddenite, Highlands, Little Switzerland (2), Marshall, Spruce Pine (3) (FT); Nevada: Ely; Virginia: Virginia City (SA); Washington: Ravensdale (GS)
  Almandine garnets Maine: Poland (GS); Nevada: Ely
  Pyrope garnets North Carolina: Franklin
  Rhodolite garnets North Carolina: Franklin (5)

Third: Pearl No listing

Fourth: Blue Topaz No listing

Fifth: Sapphire Georgia: Cleveland, Dahlonega (SA); Montana: Alder (O), Clinton (GS), Gem Mountain, Hamilton, Helena (2), Philipsburg; North Carolina (*): Almond, Boone (SA), Canton, Cherokee, Franklin (12), Hiddenite, Little Switzerland (2), Spruce Pine; Virginia: Virginia City (SA)

Sixth: Amethyst Arizona: Glendale (GS); Arkansas: Murfreesboro (S); Georgia: Cleveland, Helen (SA); Maine: Bethel (R), West Paris; Montana: Dillon; Nevada: Reno (GS), Sun Valley (GS) (crystal scepters); New Hampshire: Grafton (I), Laconia; New Mexico: Bingham; North Carolina (*): Boone (SA), Cherokee, Chimney Rock (SA), Franklin (4), Highlands, Little Switzerland, Spruce Pine (3)
  Amethyst sceptors Arizona: Tempe

Seventh: Onyx No listing

Eighth: Tourmaline Arizona: Tempe; California: Mesa Grande; Maine: Auburn (2), Poland (GS), West Paris; North Carolina (*): Chimney Rock (SA), Franklin (6), Hiddenite, Highlands, Little Switzerland (3), Spruce Pine (3) (FT); Virginia: Amelia

    Black tourmaline California: Pala; Maine: Auburn, Bethel, Poland (GS), West Paris; New Hampshire: Grafton (I)

    Gem tourmaline Maine: West Paris

    Green tourmaline California: Pala; Maine: West Paris

    Pink tourmaline California: Pala

Ninth: Lapis Lazuli No listing

Tenth: Diamond (Jewelry) Arkansas: Murfreesboro

Eleventh: Turquoise Nevada: Reno

Twelfth: Jade No listing

Thirteenth: Citrine Georgia: Helen (SA); North Carolina (SA): Almond, Cherokee, Franklin (5), Little Switzerland, Spruce Pine (3)

Fourteenth: Opal

    Black opal Nevada: Orovado

    Common opal New Mexico: Deming

    Fire opal Nevada: Orovado, Reno (GS); Oregon: Klamath Falls

    Hyalite opal Maine: Bethel

    Precious opal Idaho: Spencer; Texas: Alpine

    Virgin Valley Nevada: Reno (GS)

    Wood opal Nevada: Denio

Fifteenth: Ruby California: Pine Grove; Georgia: Cleveland, Dahlonega (SA); Montana: Helena (R); North Carolina (*): Almond, Boone (SA), Cherokee, Chimney Rock (SA), Franklin (12), Highlands, Little Switzerland (2), Spruce Pine (3); Virginia: Virginia City (SA)

Twentieth: Emerald Georgia: Cleveland, Dahlonega (SA); North Carolina (*): Almond, Boone (SA), Cherokee, Chimney Rock, Franklin (1), Hiddenite, Little Switzerland (4), Marion, Micaville (FT), Spruce Pine (1) (also crabtree emerald)

Twenty-fifth: Silver Michigan: Hubbell

Thirtieth: Pearl No listing

Thirty-fifth: Emerald Georgia: Cleveland, Dahlonega (SA); North Carolina (*): Almond, Boone (SA), Cherokee, Chimney Rock (SA), Franklin, Hiddenite, Little Switzerland (2), Marion, Micaville (FT), Spruce Pine (1) (also crabree emerald)

Fortieth: Ruby California: Pine Grove; Georgia: Cleveland, Dahlonega (SA); Montana: Helena (R); North Carolina (*): Almond, Boone (SA), Cherokee, Chimney Rock (SA), Franklin (12), Highlands, Little Switzerland (2), Spruce Pine (3)

Forty-fifth: Sapphire Georgia: Cleveland, Dahlonega (SA); Montana: Alder, Clinton (GS), Gem Mountain, Hamilton, Helena (2), Philipsburg; North Carolina (*): Almond, Boone (SA), Canton, Cherokee, Chimney Rock (SA), Franklin (11), Hiddenite, Highlands, Little Switzerland (2), Spruce Pine; Virginia: Viginia City (SA)

Fiftieth: Gold Alaska: Fairbanks (3); Arizona: Apache Junction, Goldfield, Prescott, Wickenburg; California: Angels Camp, Coloma, Columbia, Jackson, Jamestown, Mariposa, Nevada City, Pine Grove, Placerville; Colorado: Idaho Springs (2); Georgia: Cleveland, Dahlonega (2), Gainesville, Helen; Idaho: Moscow (GS); Indiana: Knightstown; Montana: Alder (O), Helena; North Carolina: Cherokee, Marion, New London, Stanfield, Union Mills; South Dakota: Deadwood, Keystone, Lead; Virginia: Virginia City (SA)

Fifty-fifth: Alexandrite No listing

Sixtieth: Diamond Arkansas: Murfreesboro

Finding Your Zodiac Stone

The following is a listing of fee dig sites contained in this four-volume guide where you can find the stone that is associated with a particular zodiac sign. Refer to the individual mine listings for more information.

Aquarius (January 21–February 21) Garnet   Arizona: Tempe; California: Pala; Connecticut: Roxbury; Georgia: Dahlonega (SA), Helen (SA); Idaho: St. Maries; Maine: Auburn, Bethel, Poland (GS), West Paris; Montana: Alder, Helena (S); New Hampshire: Grafton (I); New Mexico: Dixon; New York: North River; North Carolina (*): Almond, Boone (SA), Cherokee, Chimney Rock (SA), Franklin (6), Hiddenite, Highlands, Little Switzerland (2), Marshall, Spruce Pine (3) (FT); Nevada: Ely; Virginia: Virginia City (SA); Washington: Ravensdale (GS)
Almandine garnets   Maine: Poland (GS); Nevada: Ely
Pyrope garnets   North Carolina: Franklin
Rhodolite garnets   North Carolina: Franklin (5)

Pisces (February 22–March 21) Amethyst   Arizona: Glendale (GS); Arkansas: Murfreesboro (S); Georgia: Cleveland, Helen (SA), Jackson's Crossroads; Maine: Albany, Bethel (R), West Paris; Montana: Dillon; Nevada: Reno (GS), Sun Valley (GS) (crystal scepters); New Hampshire: Grafton (I), Laconia; New Mexico: Bingham; New York: North River; North Carolina (*): Almond, Boone (SA), Cherokee, Chimney Rock (SA), Franklin (4), Highlands, Little Switzerland, Marion, Spruce Pine (3)
Amethyst sceptors   Arizona: Tempe

Aries (March 21–April 20) Bloodstone (green chalcedony with red spots)   No listing

Taurus (April 21–May 21) Sapphire   Georgia: Cleveland, Dahlonega (SA); Montana: Alder (O), Clinton (GS), Gem Mountain, Hamilton, Helena (2), Philipsburg; North Carolina (*): Almond, Boone (SA), Canton, Cherokee, Chimney Rock, Franklin (11), Hiddenite, Highlands, Little Switzerland (2), Spruce Pine; Virginia: Virginia City (SA)

Gemini (May 22–June 21) Agate   Arkansas: Murfreesboro(S); Iowa: Bonaporte; Montana: Helena (S); Nevada: Gerlach; New Mexico: Deming (GS); North Carolina: Chimney Rock (SA); Oklahoma: Kenton (2); Oregon: Yachats; South Dakota: Wall; Texas: Three Rivers; Virginia: Amelia
Banded agate   Texas: Alpine
Fire agate   Arizona: Safford (2)
Iris agate   Texas: Alpine

Ledge agate Oregon: Madras

Moss agate Oregon: Madras, Mitchell; Texas: Alpine (2),Wyoming: Shell

Polka-dot jasp-agate Oregon: Madras

Plume agate Nevada: Reno (GS); Oregon: Madras

Pompom agate Texas: Alpine

Rainbow agate Oregon: Madras

Red plume agate Texas: Alpine

Cancer (June 22–July 22) Emerald Georgia: Cleveland, Dahlonega (SA); North Carolina (*): Almond, Boone (SA), Cherokee, Chimney Rock (SA), Franklin, Hiddenite, Little Switzerland (2), Micaville (FT), Spruce Pine (1)

    Crabtree emerald North Carolina: Spruce Pine

Leo (July 23–August 22) Onyx No listing

Virgo (August 23–September 22) Carnelian No listing

Libra (September 23–October 23) Chrysolite or Peridot:

    Peridot Arkansas: Murfreesboro (S); North Carolina (*): Franklin

Scorpio (October 24–November 21) Beryl Georgia: LaGrange; Maine: Poland (GS), West Paris; New Mexico: Dixon; North Carolina (*): Little Switzerland (2), Spruce Pine (2); Virginia: Amelia (2)

    Aqua beryl New Hampshire: Grafton (I)

    Blue beryl New Hampshire: Grafton (I)

    Clear beryl California: Pala

    Golden beryl North Carolina: Spruce Pine (FT); New Hampshire: Grafton (I)

Sagittarius (November 22–December 21) Topaz Georgia: Cleveland, Helen (SA); Maine: Poland (GS); Montana: Helena (R); New Hampshire: Grafton (I); North Carolina (SA): Boone (SA), Cherokee, Franklin (5), Highlands, Little Switzerland (3), Spruce Pine (3); Texas: Mason; Virginia: Amelia

    Pink topaz Washington: Ravensdale (GS)

Capricorn (December 22–January 21) Ruby California: Pine Grove; Georgia: Cleveland, Dahlonega (SA); Montana: Helena (R); North Carolina (*): Almond, Boone (SA), Cherokee, Chimney Rock (SA), Franklin (12), Highlands, Little Switzerland (2), Spruce Pine (3); Virginia: Virginia City (SA)

The preceding list of zodiacal stones has been passed on from an early Hindu legend (taken from *Jewelry & Gems—The Buying Guide* by Antoinette Matlins and A. C. Bonanno, Gemstone Press, 2005).

The following is an old Spanish list, probably representing Arab traditions, which ascribes the following stones to various signs of the zodiac (taken from *Jewelry & Gems—The Buying Guide* by Antoinette Matlins and A. C. Bonanno, Gemstone Press, 2005).

Aquarius (January 21–February 21) Amethyst Arizona: Glendale (GS); Arkansas: Murfreesboro (S); Georgia: Cleveland, Helen (SA); Maine: Bethel (R), West Paris; Montana: Dillon; Nevada: Reno (GS); New Hampshire: Grafton (I), Laconia; New Mexico: Bingham; North Carolina (*): Almond, Boone (SA), Cherokee, Chimney Rock (SA), Franklin (4), Highlands, Little Switzerland, Marion, Spruce Pine (3)

Crystal scepters Nevada: Sun Valley (GS)

Amethyst scepters Arizona: Tempe

Pisces (February 22–March 21) Undistinguishable

Aries (March 21–April 20) Quartz Arizona: Glenale (GS), Tempe; Arkansas: Hot Springs, Jessieville (2), Mt. Ida (6) (Y), Murfreesboro (S), Pencil Bluff; California: Pine Grove; Colorado: Lake George; Maine: Poland (GS); Montana: Dillon, Helena; New Hampshire: Grafton; New Mexico: Bingham, Deming, Dixon, Socorro (Y); Pennsylvania: Williamsport; Texas: Alpine; Virginia: Amelia, Virginia City (SA); Washington: Ravensdale (GS)

Blue Georgia: Lincolnton; North Carolina: Marion

Clear North Carolina (*): Franklin, Hiddenite, Little Switzerland, Marion, Spruce Pine

Milky Maine: Bethel

Orange Maine: West Paris

Parallel growth Maine: West Paris

Pseudocubic crystals Maine: West Paris

Rose Georgia: Helen (SA); New Hampshire: Grafton (I); North Carolina (*): Franklin, Little Switzerland, Marion

Rose (gem quality) Maine: Albany, West Paris

Rutilated North Carolina (*): Little Switzerland, Spruce Pine

Smoky Georgia: Helen (SA); Maine: Bethel, West Paris; New Hampshire: Grafton (I); North Carolina (*): Almond, Boone (SA), Cherokee, Franklin (5), Hiddenite, Highlands, Little Switzerland (2), Marion, Spruce Pine (2)

Smoky (gem quality) Maine: West Paris

Star rose Georgia: LaGrange

Quartz "diamonds"

Lake Co. "diamonds" (moon tears) California: Lake County

Cape May "diamonds" New Jersey: Cape May

Herkimer "diamonds" New York: Herkimer, Little Falls, Middleville, St. Johnsville

Taurus (April 21–May 21) Rubies, Diamonds:

Rubies California: Pine Grove; Georgia: Dahlonega (SA); Montana: Helena (R); North Carolina (*): Almond, Cherokee, Franklin (11), Highlands, Little Switzerland (2), Spruce Pine (3)

Diamonds Arkansas: Murfreesboro

Gemini (May 22–June 21) Sapphire Georgia: Cleveland, Dahlonega (SA); Montana: Alder (O), Clinton (GS), Gem Mountain, Hamilton, Helena (2), Philipsburg; North Carolina (*): Almond, Boone (SA), Canton, Cherokee, Franklin (11), Hiddenite, Highlands, Little Switzerland (2), Spruce Pine; Virginia: Virginia City (SA)

Cancer (June 22–July 22) Agate and Beryl:

Agate Arkansas: Murfreesboro (S); Iowa: Bonaparte; Montana: Helena (S); Nevada: Gerlach; New Mexico: Deming (GS); North Carolina: Boone (SA); Oklahoma: Kenton (2); Oregon: Yachats; South Dakota: Wall; Texas: Three Rivers; Virginia: Amelia

Banded agate Texas: Alpine

Fire agate Arizona: Safford (2)

Iris agate Texas: Alpine

Ledge agate Oregon: Madras

Moss agate Oregon: Madras, Mitchell; Texas: Alpine (2), Wyoming: Shell

Polka-dot agate Oregon: Madras (R)

Plume agate Nevada: Reno (GS); Oregon: Madras

Pompom agate Texas: Alpine

Rainbow agate Oregon: Madras (R)

Red plume agate Texas: Alpine

Beryl Georgia: LaGrange; Maine: Poland (GS), West Paris; New Mexico, Dixon; North Carolina (*): Little Switzerland (2), Spruce Pine (2); Virginia: Amelia (2)

Aqua beryl New Hampshire: Grafton (I)

Blue beryl New Hampshire: Grafton (I)

Clear beryl California: Pala

Golden beryl North Carolina: Spruce Pine (FT); New Hampshire: Grafton (I)

Leo (July 23–August 22) Topaz
Georgia: Cleveland, Helen (SA); Maine: Poland (GS); Montana: Helena (R); New Hampshire: Grafton (I); North Carolina (SA): Boone (SA), Cherokee, Franklin (5), Highlands, Little Switzerland (3), Spruce Pine (3); Texas: Mason; Virginia: Amelia

Pink topaz Washington: Ravensdale (GS)

Virgo (August 23–September 22) Bloodstone (green chalcedony with red spots)
No listing

Libra (September 23–October 23) Jasper
Arkansas: Murfreesboro (S); California: Pine Grove; Montana: Helena; Oklahoma: Kenton; Oregon: Madras, Yachats; Texas: Alpine

Brown jasper New Mexico: Deming

Chocolate jasper New Mexico: Deming

Orange jasper New Mexico: Deming

Picture jasper Oregon: Mitchell

Pink jasper New Mexico: Deming

Variegated jasper New Mexico: Deming

Yellow jasper New Mexico: Deming

Scorpio (October 24–November 21) Garnet
Arizona: Tempe; California: Pala; Connecticut: Roxbury; Georgia: Dahlonega (SA), Helen (SA); Idaho: St. Maries; Maine: Auburn, Bethel, Poland (GS), West Paris; Montana: Alder, Helena (S); New

Hampshire: Grafton (I); New Mexico: Dixon; North Carolina (*): Almond, Boone (SA), Cherokee, Chimney Rock (SA), Franklin (5), Hiddenite, Highlands, Little Switzerland (2), Marshall, Spruce Pine (3) (FT); Nevada: Ely; Virginia: Virginia City; Washington: Ravensdale (GS)

Almandine garnets Maine: Poland (GS); Nevada: Ely

Pyrope garnets North Carolina: Franklin

Rhodolite garnets North Carolina: Franklin (5)

Sagittarius (November 22–December 21) Emerald Georgia: Cleveland, Dahlonega (SA); North Carolina (*): Cherokee, Franklin, Hiddenite, Little Switzerland (2), Marion, Spruce Pine (2)

Crabtree emerald North Carolina: Spruce Pine

Capricorn (December 22–January 21) Chalcedony Arizona: Safford; New Mexico: Deming

Blue chalcedony Nevada: Sun Valley (GS)

Some Publications on Gems and Minerals

Lapidary Journal

Main Office
300 Chesterfield Parkway, Suite 100
Malvern, PA 19355
Phone: (610) 232-5770
Subscriptions: (800) 676-4336
www.lapidaryjournal.com

Rocks & Minerals

Heldref Publications
1319 18th Street, NW
Washington, DC 20036-1802
Subscriptions: (800) 365-9753

Rock & Gem

c/o Miller Magazines, Inc.
Maple Court, Suite 232
Ventura, CA 93003-3517
www.rockngem.com

Gold Prospector

Gold Prospectors Association of America, Inc.
P.O. Box 891509
Temecula, CA 92589
Phone: (951) 699-4749
www.goldprospectors.org

Other sources of information are local and regional rock, gem, and mineral clubs and federations, and rock, gem, and mineral shows. Many times clubs offer field trips and some shows have collecting trips associated with their annual event.

Send Us Your Feedback

Disclaimer

The authors have made every reasonable effort to obtain accurate information for this guide. However, much of the information in the book is based on material provided by the sites and has not been verified independently. The information given here does not represent recommendations, but merely a listing of information. The authors and publisher accept no liability for any accident or loss incurred when readers are patronizing the establishments listed herein. The authors and publisher accept no liability for errors or omissions. Since sites may shut down or change their hours of operations or fees without advance notice, please call the site before your visit for confirmation before planning your trip.

The authors would appreciate being informed of changes, additions, or deletions that should be made to this guide. To that end, a form is attached, which can be filled out and mailed to the authors for use in future editions of the guide.

Have We Missed Your Mine or Museum?

This is a project with a national scope, based on extensive literature search, phone and mail inquiry, and personal investigation. However, we are dealing with a business in which many owners are retiring or closing and selling their sites. In addition, many of the mines, guide services, and smaller museums have limited publicity, known more by word of mouth than by publication. Thus, it is possible that your operation or one you have visited was not included in this guide. Please let us know if you own or operate a mine, guide service, or museum, or have visited a mine, guide service, or museum that is not in the guide. It will be considered for inclusion in the next edition of the guide. Send updates to:

Treasure Hunter's Guides
GemStone Press
Route 4, Sunset Farm Offices
P.O. Box 237
Woodstock, VT 05091

Do You Have a Rockhounding Story to Share?

If you have a special story about a favorite dig site, send it in for consideration for use in the next edition of the guide.

A Request to Mines and Museums:

For sites already included in this guide, we request that you put us on your annual mailing list so that we may have an updated copy of your information.

Notes on Museums

In this guide we have included listings of museums with noteworthy gem, mineral, or rock collections. We particularly tried to find local museums displaying gems or minerals native to the area where they are located. This list is by no means complete, and if you feel we missed an important listing, let us know by completing the following form. Since these guides focus specifically on gems and minerals, only those exhibits have been recognized in the museum listings, and we do not mention any collection or exhibits of fossils.

READER'S CONTRIBUTION

I would like to supply the following information for possible inclusion in the next edition of *The Treasure Hunter's Guide*:

Type of entry: ☐ fee dig   ☐ guide service   ☐ museum   ☐ mine tour
☐ annual event

This is a: ☐ new entry   ☐ entry currently in the guide

Nature of info: ☐ addition   ☐ change   ☐ deletion

Please describe (brochure and additional info may be attached):

_____

_____

_____

_____

Please supply the following in case we need to contact you regarding your information:

Name: _____

Address: _____

_____

_____

Phone: (_____) _____

E-mail: _____

Date: _____

DIAMONDS, 2ND EDITION:
THE ANTOINETTE MATLINS BUYING GUIDE
How to Select, Buy, Care for & Enjoy Diamonds with Confidence and Knowledge
by Antoinette Matlins, P.G.

Practical, comprehensive, and easy to understand, this book includes price guides for old and new cuts and for fancy-color, treated, and synthetic diamonds. **Explains in detail** how to read diamond grading reports and offers important advice for after buying a diamond. **The "unofficial bible" for all diamond buyers who want to get the most for their money.**

6" x 9", 220 pp., 12 full-color pages & many b/w illustrations and photos; index
Quality Paperback Original, ISBN 0-943763-46-0 **$18.99**

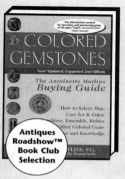

COLORED GEMSTONES, 2ND EDITION:
THE ANTOINETTE MATLINS BUYING GUIDE
How to Select, Buy, Care for & Enjoy Sapphires, Emeralds, Rubies and Other Colored Gems with Confidence and Knowledge
by Antoinette Matlins, P.G.

This practical, comprehensive, easy-to-understand guide **provides in depth** all the information you need to buy colored gems with confidence. Includes price guides for popular gems, opals, and synthetic stones. Provides examples of gemstone grading reports and offers important advice for after buying a gemstone. **Shows anyone shopping for colored gemstones how to get the most for their money.**

6" x 9", 224 pp., 24 full-color pages & many b/w illustrations and photos; index
Quality Paperback Original, ISBN 0-943763-45-2 **$18.99**

THE PEARL BOOK, 3RD EDITION:
THE DEFINITIVE BUYING GUIDE
How to Select, Buy, Care for & Enjoy Pearls
by Antoinette Matlins, P.G.
COMPREHENSIVE • EASY TO READ • PRACTICAL

This comprehensive, authoritative guide tells readers everything they need to know about pearls to fully understand and appreciate them, and avoid any unexpected—and costly—disappointments, now and in future generations.

- A journey into the rich history and romance surrounding pearls.
- The five factors that determine pearl value & judging pearl quality.
- What to look for, what to look out for: How to spot fakes. Treatments.
- Differences between natural, cultured and imitation pearls, and ways to separate them.
- Comparisons of all types of pearls, in every size and color, from every pearl-producing country.

6" x 9", 232 pp., 16 full-color pages & over 250 color and b/w illustrations and photos; index
Quality Paperback, ISBN 0-943763-35-5 **$19.99**

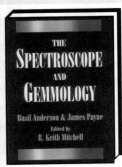

Buy Your *"Tools of the Trade"*...

Gem Identification Instruments directly from *GemStone Press*

Whatever instrument you need, GemStone Press can help.
Use our convenient order form, or contact us directly for assistance.

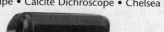
ITEM / QUANTITY	PRICE EA.*	TOTAL $
Pocket Instrument Sets		
_____ **Premium:** With Bausch & Lomb 10X Loupe • RosGem Dichroscope • Chelsea Filter	$197.95	$ _____
_____ **Deluxe:** With Bausch & Lomb 10X Loupe • EZview Dichroscope • Chelsea Filter	$179.95	_____
Loupes—Professional Jeweler's 10X Triplet Loupes		
_____ Bausch & Lomb 10X Triplet Loupe	$44.00	_____
_____ Standard 10X Triplet Loupe	$29.00	_____
_____ Darkfield Loupe	$58.95	_____
• Spot filled diamonds, identify inclusions in colored gemstones. Operates with mini maglite (optional).		
Analyzer		
_____ Gem Analyzer (RosGem)	$299.00	_____
• Combines Darkfield Loupe, Polariscope, and Immersion Cell. Operates with mini maglite (optional).		
Calcite Dichroscopes		
_____ Dichroscope (RosGem)	$135.00	_____
_____ Dichroscope (EZview)	$115.00	_____
Color Filters		
_____ Chelsea Filter	$44.95	_____
_____ Synthetic Emerald Filter Set (Hanneman)	$32.00	_____
_____ Tanzanite Filter (Hanneman)	$28.00	_____
_____ Bead Buyer's & Parcel Picker's Filter Set (Hanneman)	$24.00	_____
Diamond Testers and Tweezers		
_____ SSEF Diamond-Type Spotter	$150.00	_____
_____ Diamondnite Dual Tester	$269.00	_____
_____ Diamond Tweezers/Locking	$10.65	_____
_____ Diamond Tweezers/Non-Locking	$7.80	_____
Jewelry Cleaners		
_____ Ionic Cleaner—Home size model	$69.95	_____
_____ Ionic Solution—16 oz. bottle	$20.00	_____

Buy Your "Tools of the Trade..."

Gem Identification Instruments directly from *GemStone Press*

Whatever instrument you need, GemStone Press can help.
Use our convenient order form, or contact us directly for assistance.

ITEM / QUANTITY	PRICE EA.*	TOTAL $
Lamps—Ultraviolet & High Intensity		
_____ Small Longwave/Shortwave (UVP)	$72.00	_____
_____ Large Longwave/Shortwave (UVP)	$199.95	_____
_____ Viewing Cabinet for Large Lamp (UVP)	$175.00	_____
_____ **Purchase Large Lamp & Cabinet together and save $35.00**	$339.95	_____
_____ SSEF High-Intensity Shortwave Illuminator • For Use with the SSEF Diamond-Type Spotter	$499.00	
Other Light Sources		
_____ Solitaire Maglite	$11.00	_____
_____ Mini Maglite	$15.00	_____
_____ Flex Light	$29.95	_____
Refractometers		
_____ Precision Pocket Refractometer (RosGem RFA 322) • operates with solitaire maglite (additional—see above)	$625.00	_____
_____ Refractive Index Liquid 1.81—10 gram	$59.95	_____
Spectroscopes		
_____ Spectroscope—Pocket-sized model (OPL)	$98.00	_____
_____ Spectroscope—Desk model w/stand (OPL)	$235.00	_____
Scale		
_____ GemPro50 Carat Scale	$174.95	_____

Shipping/Insurance per order in the U.S.: $7.95 first item, $3.00 each add'l item; $10.95 total for pocket instrument set.   SHIPPING/INS. $_____

Outside the U.S.: Please specify *insured* shipping method you prefer and provide a credit card number for payment.   **TOTAL $ _____****

Check enclosed for $ _____ (Payable to: GEMSTONE PRESS)
Charge my credit card: ❏ Visa ❏ MasterCard
Name on Card _____ Phone (_____)_____
Cardholder Address: Street _____
City/State/Zip _____ E-mail _____
Credit Card # _____ Exp. Date _____
Signature _____ CID # _____
Please send to: ❏ Same as Above ❏ Address Below
Name _____
Street _____
City/State/Zip _____ Phone (_____)_____

Phone, mail, fax, or e-mail orders to:

GEMSTONE PRESS, P.O. Box 237, Woodstock, VT 05091
Tel: (802) 457-4000 • *Fax:* (802) 457-4004
Credit Card Orders: (800) 962-4544 (8:30AM–5:30PM ET Monday–Friday)
sales@gemstonepress.com • www.gemstonepress.com
Generous Discounts on Quantity Orders

TOTAL SATISFACTION GUARANTEE
If for any reason you're not completely delighted with your purchase, return it in resellable condition within 30 days for a full refund.

*Prices, manufacturing specifications, and terms subject to change without notice. Orders accepted subject to availability.

**All orders must be prepaid by credit card, money order or check in U.S. funds drawn on a U.S. bank.

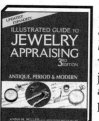
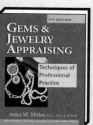